THE LUCKY DOG
WEIGHT LOSS PLAN

Vicky Marshall is an author and co-founder of
Honey's Real Dog Food – a family business based in
rural Wiltshire that combines animal welfare with
ethically produced British ingredients to provide a
nutritionally balanced diet for dogs.

THE LUCKY DOG WEIGHT LOSS PLAN

WHY YOU NEVER SEE A FAT WOLF

VICKY MARSHALL

an imprint of Head of Zeus

First published in the UK in 2017 by Anima,
an imprint of Head of Zeus

Copyright © Vicky Marshall, 2017

9 7 5 3 1 2 4 6 8

A catalogue record for this book is available
from the British Library

ISBN (TPB): 9781786697448
ISBN (E): 9781786697431

Images pages iii, 13, 25 (both), 64, 65, 73, 76, 78, 80, 94,
115 (both), 143, 148, 218 (both) courtesy of Honey's.
Images pages 8, 13, 103, 122, 139, 202, 224 © Shutterstock.
Images pages 24, 123, 137 © Alamy. Images pages 42, 55, 123,
163, 170 © Getty Images. Images pages 102, 103 © iStock

Designed by Nicola Moseley
Printed and bound in Italy by Lego S.p.a.

Head of Zeus Ltd
First Floor East
5–8 Hardwick Street
London EC1R 4RG
www.headofzeus.com

For my darling family: Gary, James, Kate and Harry…
and our own 'Lucky Dogs' Rudi-Doodle and Fletcher

CONTENTS

FOREWORD

When I qualified as a vet in 1973 and was therefore entitled to put the letters MRCVS (Member of the Royal College of Veterinary Surgeons) after my name, the world was a very different place, and veterinary practice was a very different world.

If you were sitting in the waiting room of your local vet in 1973, two things would have been strikingly different from the waiting room of your vet today. Firstly, the sales area (had there been one) was not packed from floor to ceiling with pet food. Secondly, there were very few obese dogs amongst the throng of pets waiting to see the vet.

Over the years, and over the last couple of decades in particular, there has been a phenomenal growth in the number of obese dogs. Why is this so? It may be true that some dogs are getting insufficient exercise, but the increase in obesity has mirrored the increase in the feeding of high-carbohydrate, low-quality protein, processed diets. I don't believe this can be a coincidence.

Dogs in the seventies were mainly fed on scraps, leftovers, bones and cheap meat and offal from the local butcher. There were few dog treats available and most dogs had plenty of walks and runs. Obesity was rare.

Dogs today are commonly fed on kibble, a form of dried food that is high in fats (to give it some taste) and in carbohydrates, and low in high-quality protein. Essentially, this is junk food for dogs. Most canned foods are little better, some containing as little as three or four per cent real meat.

There is a plethora of dog treats on the market. And obesity is common.

Dogs are carnivores. They have evolved to eat meat, offal, raw bones and vegetables. Dogs are social animals. They are designed to have lots of play and interaction with other dogs and with their human companions. If they eat what they have evolved to eat and are given the physical and mental stimulation they need, they will not get overweight.

It's as simple as that.

One caveat – some medical conditions, such as hypothyroidism, Cushing's disease, diabetes and others, can cause a dog to become overweight. Hypothyroidism (an underactive thyroid) is often hard to diagnose, and there are probably quite a number of obese dogs that have an underlying thyroid imbalance.

If your dog is becoming obese, and does not have a medical condition that may be causing the weight gain, what can you do about it? Your local vet may well have a weight control clinic. You can take your dog for a regular weigh-in, and will be given advice about nutrition by a practice nurse, who will probably have a qualification in canine nutrition. Should you enquire about this qualification, it will almost certainly be a certificate or diploma granted by one of the major pet food manufacturers. For instance, many veterinary nurses are 'Hills Pet Nutrition Advisers'. Hills is a multi national conglomerate that sells a range of processed dog foods, especially kibbles, sponsors many veterinary meetings and advertises heavily to the veterinary profession. There are several other multinationals that do much the same. Some provide free food to veterinary colleges and to animal a more traditional, more natural diet: the same sort of diet that our great-grandparents fed to their dogs. The same sort of diet, in fact, that wolves and wild dogs eat. Dogs, as I explain below, have a digestive system identical to that of the grey wolf (not so surprising given that they are so closely related they can interbreed) and flourish on the same diet. It is thanks to this diet that you never, ever see an overweight wolf, no matter how much he or she eats.

Implementing such a diet is simplicity itself, which is why this book is relatively short. Moreover, not only will your dog adore the change, but also his or her excess weight will fall away as if by magic. This will bring about another benefit: better health. All the research indicates that dogs who are the correct weight suffer less illness and disease.

What Is The Lucky Dog Weight Loss Plan?

I developed the Lucky Dog Weight Loss Plan through observation and experiment, but my findings reflect extensive scientific research. The predominant components of the Lucky Dog Weight Loss Plan are high in protein, low in carbohydrate and contain the right quantity of 'good' fat.

I have spent the last eight years providing thousands of dogs a raw food diet through my business – Honey's Real Dog Food. It took me a while to notice, but I began to realise that none of my canine customers who were fed to our guidelines were overweight. This was during a time when pet obesity was on the increase with over 50% of

01

INTRODUCING THE LUCKY DOG WEIGHT LOSS PLAN

The old ways are sometimes the best ways. A hundred years ago, even fifty years ago, very few dogs had weight issues. Whatever they were doing or being fed, it wasn't affecting their collar sizes or their waistlines. Today, however, approximately half of British dogs are either overweight or obese.

What has happened to bring about this change?

Certainly, it doesn't help that society as a whole has become more sedentary or that legislation means that a dog can no longer get extra exercise by roaming freely around the neighbourhood where he or she lives.

It is possible, too, that dogs have become more persuasive when asking for extra food and treats.

However, I am certain, based on my experience of feeding several thousand dogs a month, that the main cause is modern dog food. Modern dog food is high in simple carbohydrate, low in protein and full of harmful fats – the perfect recipe if you want to push a dog's weight up.

Indeed, it is no coincidence that within a few years of the formula being developed, a growing number of dogs began to pile on the pounds.

Thankfully, the effects of modern dog food are quickly reversed. If there is a dog in your life who isn't quite as slim or svelte as you would like, the solution is straightforward. All you have to do is feed your four-legged family member

01

INTRODUCING THE LUCKY DOG WEIGHT LOSS PLAN

charities, and some have actually paid the salaries of vets who lecture students on nutrition at veterinary colleges.

It seems unlikely that a major pet food company can train a veterinary nurse in nutrition without just a smidgen of bias towards their own products – which are likely to be expensive and, in my view, entirely unnecessary 'therapeutic' weight-reduction diet foods.

Vicky Marshall explains clearly and straightforwardly what dogs should be eating, how their digestive systems work, why they can become obese, and how to get them back on track if they are getting overweight.

Lucky indeed is the dog that benefits from the wisdom and common sense of the Lucky Dog Weight Loss Plan.

Richard Allport
BVet Med. Vet MFHom MRCVS

pet dogs with weight problems. With two male, castrated, Labrador X breeds … keeping trim is an important on-going part of my life too !

Because modern, processed dog food has very low levels of very poor-quality protein (often from vegetable sources, which dogs can't absorb), manufacturers have done their best to persuade everyone that protein is not good for a dog.

In fact, high-quality, animal protein is exactly what your dog needs to thrive. The secret is to give your dog the same levels that he or she would enjoy if they decided, as a result of seeing too many disaster movies, to leave home and become self-sufficient survivalists, living in the wilderness and fending for themselves.

This would vary from meal to meal, of course, as I explain later on. The real point I want to make now is that the natural level of protein found in the diet I am recommending is perfect for your dog.

It can take as little as two weeks for an overweight dog to achieve meaningful weight loss on this diet, although I generally suggest that you don't rush the process and allow between 60 and 90 days, or longer. One of the many benefits of the diet is that it leads to the loss of fat, not muscle mass, which is much healthier for your dog. Independent research, incidentally, has shown that the two main components of the Lucky Dog Weight Loss Plan leave dogs feeling fuller than a wide range of alternative ingredients.

Honey's

If you read this book through to the end you will find a chapter about my own business: Honey's Real Dog Food. We have a policy at Honey's of providing free diet and health advice to anyone who contacts us, even if they never intend to become a customer. Please do get in touch if we can be of any assistance. We have a special team that looks after poorly and/or overweight dogs.

When to seek experienced help

There are circumstances when a switch to the Lucky Dog Weight Loss Plan should only be undertaken with experienced guidance. Dogs that have recently undergone bowel surgery or chemotherapy or who have a compromised immune system can all benefit from the Lucky Dog Weight Loss Plan but may need a special diet. Also, pregnant dogs and new mums will have special nutritional needs. Please do contact us at Honey's for free advice (you don't have to be a customer) or consult a vet or other professional with relevant expertise (see Chapter 13 for a list of vets who have approved and support the Lucky Dog Weight Loss Plan).

A Bluffer's Guide To The Lucky Dog Weight Loss Plan

Pressed for time but keen to understand the basics of the Lucky Dog Weight Loss Plan? Here is a summary of all the main points made in this book.

Half the dogs in the UK are either overweight or obese

Why? Lack of exercise plays a role, but the main reason is modern dog food. Over the last few decades manufacturers have switched to a formula that is making it difficult for dogs to stay trim, namely low levels of protein, high levels of simple carbohydrate and an excess of unhealthy fats.

Problems with modern, processed dog food

• It is cooked. Cooking destroys 70% of the nutritional value of the food from a dog's perspective and makes it exceedingly difficult to digest

• It can contain inappropriate and damaging chemicals (binders, colouring, preservatives and other additives)

• The quality of t he ingredients is usually poor. Even expensive dog food often has very low-quality ingredients

- Most dog foods contain a high percentage of grain (including rice), which is unsuitable for the canine digestive system and causes allergies

- 'Grain-free' dry food might be free from grain, but it won't be free of carbohydrates such as potato, sweet potato, lentils, peas (pea starch), chickpeas, tapioca or another carbohydrate source(s). Carbohydrates can lead to blood sugar fluctuations, insulin resistance, obesity, diabetes and other health problems in dogs

- It generally fails to clean the dog's teeth and gums, allowing plaque to build up. This gives rise to periodontal disease and worse

Modern dog food is high in simple carbohydrate, low in protein and full of harmful fats – the perfect recipe if you want to push a dog's weight up.

Dogs share the identical digestive system to the grey wolf and flourish on the same diet. It is thanks to this diet that you never, ever see an overweight wolf.

Dogs should eat a natural diet

The quick, easy and pleasurable way for dogs to lose weight is to switch from modern, processed dog food to the same sort of diet they ate a hundred (and even as recently as fifty) years ago. Such a diet is high in natural protein, low in carbohydrate and includes the right balance of 'good' fats. It's the same diet that wolves eat in the wild. This is not a coincidence! Dogs and wolves are so closely related that they possess identical digestive systems and can even interbreed. Once dogs switch to a traditional, natural diet the weight falls off them, as if by magic. Best of all, they really love the food because it is full of extra flavour and texture.

Why the Lucky Dog Weight Loss Plan is so effective

The Lucky Dog Weight Loss Plan features what is generally referred to as a 'biologically appropriate diet'. Every creature on earth needs a specific range of foods to survive and prosper: a panda, for example, must eat bamboo. Otherwise, it will get ill and may (if the diet is really inappropriate) die. For the first four million years of dogs' existence on earth they certainly didn't eat canned food or kibble. Four million years? Yes, that's how long wolves have been around, and dogs and wolves are classified as the same species. When wolves were domesticated (around 8,000 to 20,000 years ago), we humans changed their outer appearance through breedi ng, but not their internal organs or digestive systems.

The Lucky Dog Weight Loss Plan is easy

The Lucky Dog Weight Loss Plan requires very little preparation (literally a couple of minutes a day), the instructions are simple and all the ingredients you need are available from your supermarket or butcher. The main ingredients may surprise you – raw meat, raw bone and fresh vegetables – but when you think about what wolves and dogs would eat in the wild, the rationale for the diet becomes apparent. The diet is suitable for any dog and it leads to loss of unnecessary fat, not valuable muscle mass.

The Lucky Dog Weight Loss Plan has long-term benefits

Having slimmed your dog down to the correct weight using the Lucky Dog Weight Loss Plan, there is every reason to carry on feeding him or her the same diet. As those who have switched their dogs to a natural diet will testify, the results can be amazing. Benefits include a glossy coat, healthy skin, lean muscle tone, a robust immune system, sweet-smelling breath, healthy teeth and gums, increased energy, better digestion and a strong heart. Dogs eating a natural diet can be expected to live longer and to suffer less illness and disease.

02

WHY MODERN DOGS
HAVE WEIGHT ISSUES

02

WHY MODERN DOGS HAVE WEIGHT ISSUES

Dogs are wrestling with their weight for the first time in four million years. The most recent research (LVS, November 2016) into this was conducted by the Pet Food Manufacturers' Association (PFMA), which found that 49 out of every 100 British dogs were either overweight or obese, a substantial increase on the previous survey. The organisation called upon pet owners to 'resist overfeeding and excessive treating'.

The PFMA is in a difficult position. On the one hand, it is moving with the times and counts amongst its membership a growing number of raw dog food producers. On the other hand, some of its members could be considered part of the problem, not part of the solution. Modern, processed dog food, with its lack of protein and high levels of carbohydrates and unhealthy fats, is the single most important reason why our canine companions are becoming chubbier.

Moreover, processed dog food manufacturers, never slow to see a business opportunity, have now developed special 'weight loss' dog foods to correct a situation largely of their own making. These diet foods, incidentally, tend to be packed with crude fibre (such as beet pulp or peanut shells), which has the effect of filling a dog up without offering it any nutrition whatsoever.

Nature Knows Best

What dog food manufacturers are trying to do, in their warped way, is replicate a natural diet using inexpensive and often inappropriate ingredients. Modern dog food is highly processed and, almost without exception, utilises poor-quality ingredients, which, through methods such as cooking and extrusion, have lost most of whatever nutritional value they may ever have contained. What we are talking about is junk food for dogs. The best way for any species (including humans) to get their nutrition is in its most natural form.

What Dogs Eat When Given The Choice

The best way to understand the shortcomings of modern, processed dog food is to compare it with a dog's biologically appropriate diet (the food it must have to optimise its health). Happily, we have two ways of knowing what this is. First, there has been a lot of research into what wild dogs (such as dingoes in Australia) eat when they have complete freedom of choice. Second, domesticated dogs and wolves have identical digestive systems from their teeth to – ahem – their tails. As they are the same species, this isn't so surprising, and it provides scientific proof as to why they should be eating the same diet.

What do wild dogs and wolves eat? Small and medium-sized prey animals such as mice, voles, rabbits, birds and (where available) fish. They consume every bit of the animal, too, including the bones (which supply about a third of their nutritional requirements) and the stomach contents. They also scavenge, eating a wide variety of grasses, herbs, vegetables and fruits as well as less appetising things such as faeces.

Why your dog's weight is such a big issue

Does it really matter if your dog is carrying a little extra weight? If you care about your dog's health then the answer is 'yes'. Excess weight will reduce your dog's life expectancy and will make him or her prone to all sorts of serious health problems including (but not only) joint disease, arthritis, heart disease, hypertension, respiratory problems, asthma, pancreatitis, diabetes, liver disease, skin issues, cancer and a compromised immune system.

An Analysis Of A Dog's Natural Diet

A canine nutrition expert called Steve Brown has analysed what wild dogs and wolves eat in order to ascertain what domesticated dogs require. After extracting the water (in other words on a 'dry matter' basis) he found that the dog's calorie intake from a natural diet comes from:

- 49% protein
- 44% fat
- 6%   carbohydrate

By the way, please remember that calorie intake is different from volume of food. For example, although 44% of calories come from fat, in terms of volume of food fat only accounts for around 6% of the dog's diet. This is because fat is so calorie rich.

Modern, Processed Dog Food Doesn't Stack Up That Well

How does modern, processed dog food compare to a dog's natural diet? This can be difficult to judge, since the law allows manufacturers to present the ingredients they use in a very misleading way. For example, they can hide the percentage of carbohydrates and disguise the volume and type of fat. However, my own research suggests the following averages:

	PROTEIN	FAT	CARBO HYDRATE
NATURAL OR WILD DIET	49%	44%	6%
DRY FOOD I.E. KIBBLE	27%	30%	43%
CANNED FOOD	32%	58%	10%

You'll notice that modern dog food is low in protein and high in carbohydrate. This is the opposite of a dog's natural diet. The fat content is low or high depending on whether you feed kibble or canned food, but either way it is harmful, as manufacturers use inappropriate and unhealthy fat.

The Importance Of Protein

Why is the amount of protein in your dog's diet so important? And does it matter what the source of that protein is?

Protein is what your dog needs to form critical body parts in order to remain healthy, for example cells, protective tissue, hormones and enzymes, plus tendons and ligaments. It is essential for a good immune system and the mainstay of a wolf's or wild dog's natural diet, accounting for around 90% of what it eats and providing around half the calories it requires. Research published in 2010 shows that a high-protein diet has the additional advantage of making a dog feel fuller.

However, there is protein and there is protein! In a natural diet it comes almost completely from animal sources (meat and fish), which, unlike the vast majority of plants, contain the right balance of amino acids as well as a complete range of protein-type nutrients (e.g. taurine and carnitine).

The protein in modern, processed dog food has various drawbacks. To begin with, it has, of course, been cooked. The main constituents of protein, amino acids, are altered and can be destroyed by heat. Even if the proteins survive the rendering process (when they are, essentially, boiled for a long period of time) they are of low quality, being from factory-farmed animals. Also, some modern dog food relies on lesser, plant-based proteins.

What the experts say about protein

'Research shows that a high-protein, low-carbohydrate diet is the safest and most effective weight loss programme for dogs,' say Jean Hofve DVM and Dr Celeste Yarnall, authors of *Paleo Dog*.

'Protein,' says Dr Lew Olson, author of *Raw and Natural Nutrition for Dogs*, 'is a dog's best friend.' She goes on to point out that: 'Recent studies have confirmed that a high level of protein is not just beneficial, but necessary for dogs of all ages.'

'Protein,' according to Steve Brown, author of *Unlocking the Canine Ancestral Diet*, 'provided 49% of the calories in the dog's ancestral diet, our gold standard.'

'Protein,' says Dr Karen Becker, author of *Real Food for Healthy Dogs and Cats*, 'is the foundation of the diet of a carnivore, necessary for the formation of healthy cells, enzymes, hormones, ligaments, tendons, organs and protective tissue. Next to water, it makes up the majority of our pet's body weight.'

'To maximize our pets' health,' says Dr Ian Billinghurst, author of *The BARF Diet: Raw Feeding for Dogs and Cats Using Evolutionary Methods* (and other titles), 'we should supply our pets with protein that mimics the protein eaten by their wild ancestors.'

Once dogs switch to a traditional, natural diet the weight falls off them, as if by magic. They aren't hungry and they will lose unwanted fat not valuable muscle mass.

The Lucky Dog Weight Loss Plan takes a couple of minutes a day to prepare. The main ingreditents are raw meat, raw bone and fresh vegetables, which is what wolves and dogs eat in the wild.

Yes, there are dogs who, like Oscar Wilde, can resist anything but temptation. But the underlying problem is that modern dog food is fattening.

The Importance Of Fat

Fats break down into three different types: saturated fats, monounsaturated fats and polyunsaturated fats. In their natural state in animals these come from muscle meat, storage fat, bone marrow and organ fat. By feeding your dog different types of meat you make sure that he or she receives the right quantity of 'good' fats in their most natural state.

Fat is a vital part of your dog's diet. First and foremost, fat produces energy. The right sorts of fats are necessary for the absorption of fat-soluble vitamins. Additionally, they protect the nerve fibres in the body, provide protection from the cold, and are the ideal source of essential fatty acids. They are anti-inflammatory, too. The most important fatty acids for a dog are omega-6 and omega-3.

The fat you serve your dog should be fresh. Rancid and poor-quality fats can really harm dogs, robbing them of essential fatty acids. The fat used in modern, processed dog food is of the poorest quality and comes from a variety of sources including the waste fat left over from fast food businesses. It has almost no nutritional value and is the single most important reason why dogs put on weight. Where extra fats (such as fish oils, a vital source of omegas) are added to factory-produced dog food they are generally rancid by the time the food is eaten. This is because as soon as fat comes into contact with air it starts to oxidise. The more rancid a fat, the less valuable it is as it will have the effect of reducing the nutritional value of the protein, vitamins and antioxidants so necessary to your dog's health.

So, the rules with fat are: a) you must avoid the damaging fats in modern, processed dog food and b) even though a dog may be trying to lose weight you shouldn't cut out fat completely, only reduce the quantity.

The Problem With Carbohydrates

What is wrong with feeding a dog carbohydrates? Simple carbohydrates (such as rice, barley and oats) increase blood sugar, stimulate the production of pre-inflammatory hormones and (in plain English) play merry hell with a dog's immune system. There is another problem, which is that dogs lack the digestive system required to convert most carbohydrates into a form they can actually use. Modern, processed dog food is very high in carbohydrates and the worst thing is that they are high-fibre carbohydrates. The cellulose in the fibre can't be digested (it goes in one end and out the other) and the starches reduce the body's ability to absorb other vital nutrients, such as calcium, magnesium, zinc and iron. A growing number of vets believe that it is the high levels of carbohydrates in modern dog food that are making so many dogs vulnerable to illness and disease.

It Isn't Just The Food

There is, of course, another reason why dogs are becoming overweight: lack of exercise. Society has become increasingly pressured and many people find themselves without the necessary time or energy to walk their dogs as much as they would wish. Most breeds need a minimum of an hour a day, but the PFMA says that only about a third of dogs are receiving this level. There is another problem, too. In the old days dogs were allowed to roam relatively freely. Even where this was against the local authority's regulations, a blind eye would be turned to the practice of turning dogs out for part or all of the day. My memory may be faulty, but I had no sense growing up that there were more cases of dogs biting people than there are now. Rather, I remember a society that was much more dog friendly. A society in which dogs frequently exercised themselves. I am not suggesting we turn the clock back, but it is another reason why dogs are more likely to be overweight.

Check for underlying health issues

If you feel that your dog's weight issues can't be properly explained by diet or lack of exercise then I would urge you to talk to your vet about whether it could be caused by thyroid issues or some type of hormonal problem.

03

THE LUCKY DOG
WEIGHT LOSS PLAN!

03

THE LUCKY DOG WEIGHT LOSS PLAN!

In this chapter, I explain how the Lucky Dog Weight Loss Plan works and provide all the information you need to transform your dog's weight.

The Benefits Of The Lucky Dog Weight Loss Plan

The Lucky Dog Weight Loss Plan is everything you could want from a diet.

It is easy to prepare

To prepare the Lucky Dog Weight Loss Plan usually takes two or three minutes, once or twice a day.

The ingredients are easy to find

It makes use of readily obtainable ingredients. Everything you need can be found in your local supermarket and/ or butcher.

Your dog will go crazy for it

Dogs love the taste and texture of the diet. You'll be making someone (with four paws) very happy!

It is approved by vets

The Lucky Dog Weight Loss Plan has been approved by over a dozen vets as being safe and effective. See Chapter 13 for a full list of vets who support this diet.

It is easy to understand

There's nothing complicated about the Lucky Dog Weight Loss Plan. Even the science is easy to understand.

You can expect rapid results

Usually you will see a meaningful difference in just 14 days (this is especially true of dogs coming off kibble). We know it is not as if your dog has to get into special clothes (such as a bikini or a morning suit) by a specific date, but still, it is nice to know that it isn't going to take months and months to see the improvement.

Your dog will lose the right sort of weight

One of the best things about the Lucky Dog Weight Loss Plan is that it leads to the loss of excess fat and not muscle mass.

Extra exercise is good but not vital

Although I strongly recommend extra exercise to speed things up and generally improve your dog's health, it isn't essential in order for the plan to succeed.

It will really improve your dog's health

In addition to the health benefits associated with being the correct weight, there are all sorts of other health benefits associated with this diet. Indeed, if you continue the diet after your dog's target weight has been achieved you can expect him or her to live a longer, healthier life.

Backed By Research

The Lucky Dog Weight Loss Plan is simplicity itself: a natural diet that is high in protein, low in carbohydrates and contains the optimum level of 'healthy' fat together with an appropriate exercise regime.

Extensive research has been done into the principles underlying the Lucky Dog Weight Loss Plan. Most notably in 2002, a team of scientists published a paper entitled *Weight Loss in Obese Dogs: Evaluation of a High-Protein, Low-Carbohydrate Diet*. Their findings were conclusive: there just isn't a better way for a dog to lose weight.

How Much Should Your Dog Weigh?

The first step when introducing the Lucky Dog Weight Loss Plan is to work out your dog's ideal weight. What you should be aiming for is 'lean'. That is to say:

- You should be able to feel your dog's ribs when you touch your fingers gently to the rib cage

- From the side the belly should be tucked up

- From above your dog should have a proper waist

The diagram explains this better than words, of course. You will note that the experts believe dogs should have a body condition score of 4.5 or 5 out of 9.

There's no magic formula for working out how many pounds or kilos your dog should be losing. Although it is easy to weigh your dog yourself there is something to be said for getting your vet to do it for you and asking, at the same time, for a target. Another benefit of involving your vet is to check that there are no underlying health issues.

Incidentally, a study by a major dog food manufacturer has shown that a dog's life expectancy is significantly improved by being the correct weight.

Timing

The beauty of the Lucky Dog Weight Loss Plan is that it isn't really time critical. That is to say, there is no need for you to set yourself the objective of slimming your dog down by a specific amount within a set period. My own experience is that an overweight dog will reach his or her target weight by six weeks, whereas an obese dog may require up to 12 weeks (or more) to get into shape. I'd urge you not to rush it.

The Role Of Exercise

There is absolutely no doubt that exercise plays a key role in weight loss. It *is* possible for your dog to reach his or her target weight without increasing the amount of exercise taken, but it will slow the whole process down. Moreover, exercise brings with it huge health benefits.

See the section 'Exercise Made Easy' in Chapter 4 for more.

The Diet!

From page one of this book I have stressed repeatedly that the perfect diet for your dog uses raw ingredients and is high in natural protein, low in carbohydrates and contains the optimum level of 'healthy' fat.

What does this mean in practice?

You will be feeding your dog ingredients from four different groups

- Group 1: Raw, lean muscle meat and organs.
- Group 2: Raw, meaty bones.
- Group 3: Raw vegetables and fruit.
- Group 4: 'Boosters' such as eggs and sardines.

How much of each? Approximately one-third raw meat, one-third raw meaty bones and one-third raw vegetables and fruit. Approximately? Yes! The percentages don't have to be 100% accurate every day, providing you balance things out over a period of a week or two. In the wild, dogs eat what is available and receive the nutrition they need over time. They most definitely don't carry scales and calorie counters around with them.

What about the 'boosters' mentioned above? These give your dog extra nutrition and vitamins and you simply add one item every other day.

Let me just spell it out again:

• Your dog's diet will consist almost entirely of raw meat, raw meaty bone and raw vegetables/fruit. This is a dog's biologically appropriate diet (think wolf!) and they thrive on it

• Every meal should consist of roughly $1/3$ raw meat, $1/3$ raw meaty bone and $1/3$ raw vegetables/ fruit

• The proportions are important but you don't have to be obsessive about it

• You can pick more than one ingredient from each group each day, although it is better not to mix protein sources. In other words, serve chicken meat with chicken bones and beef meat with beef bones

However, a bit of mixing and matching is fine if it is easier.

- You'll also be feeding a 'booster' ingredient every other day

You'll find lists of ingredients (designed to make it easier for you to shop) and sample menus later in this chapter.

Stick To Less Fatty Meats

Although your dog needs a certain level of 'good' fat in his or her diet it is important not to overdo it. For this reason, I strongly advise you to avoid fatty meats (such as lamb) and fatty cuts (such as beef with marbling in it).

How Much To Serve

Another wonderful feature of the Lucky Dog Weight Loss Plan is that you don't have to concern yourself with the number of calories in the food you are serving.

Instead you simply have to weigh all the food.

Initially, I advise anyone new to the Lucky Dog Weight Loss Plan to start by feeding his or her dog 1.5% of its body weight each day (unless it is a miniature or small dog, in which case see below).

Raw is safe

An explanation as to why all the ingredients should be served raw is offered in later chapters. In case you have been worrying, let me just say here and now it is safe to feed raw food to your dog.

Let me give you an example:

- Rex weighs 30kg
- Every day he gets 1.5% of his weight in food
- 1.5% of 30kg is 450g
- Every day Rex gets 450g of food

The 450g of food, incidentally, will consist (more or less) of one-third each meat (including offal), meaty bone and vegetable/fruit. So: 150g raw meat, 150g raw meaty bone and 150g vegetables/fruit. You can feed it all in one go but I prefer to feed it in two lots as this means the dog will burn up more calories.

Why 1.5%?

I suggest you begin by feeding 1.5% of your dog's body weight every day but if, after a week or two, you are seeing no appreciable loss in weight then you may need to drop the amount to 1%.

Miniature, toy and small breeds need more food!

Even when they are on a diet, miniature, toy and small breeds usually need more than 1.5% of their body weight a day. Below are my recommendations. If, after a week or two, you are seeing no appreciable difference in weight then you may need to drop the amount down gradually until you find a level at which your dog is starting to lose those unwanted pounds.

- 1–2kg: 7%
- 3–4kg: 5%
- 5–8kg: 3%
- 9–10kg: 2%

I must stress it is always hard to apply hard-and-fast rules for the smaller dogs. In reality, breeds such as Shih Tzu, Lhasa Apso, Maltese and Bolognese tend to be much more sedentary, so often don't need anything like as much as the normal percentage, even for maintenance. Chihuahuas, Pomeranians, Papillons and Yorkies tend to be more active and ping around all over the place, and so burn off food at a much higher rate.

How To Weigh Your Dog (And How Often To Do It)

Wriggly things, dogs, and they are not always willing to step neatly on to the scales to be weighed. The solution, if you are having a problem weighing them, is to weigh yourself holding your dog and then again not holding your dog. My arithmetic is useless but even I am pretty certain that the difference will represent the weight of your dog.

- Mrs. Smith holding Twiggy in her arms = 93kg
- Mrs. Smith all by herself = 60kg
- Twiggy = 33kg

Ideally, you should weigh your dog once a week and then adjust the daily portion size accordingly, keeping it at a steady 1.5% (or whatever percentage you have decided upon).

No Special Equipment Needed

You won't need any special equipment, just a set of kitchen scales, a blender or food processor, a cutting board and knife and a weighing scale (for humans).

Preparing The Food

The Lucky Dog Weight Loss Plan requires almost no preparation. Here are some tips.

- When you are serving meat you may like to mince it (if it isn't minced already) or cut it into cubes

- Dogs are remarkably clever at dealing with carcasses, chicken wings, meaty bones and so forth... it is the most natural food in the world for them

- The vegetables and fruit can be put through the food mixer and either juiced or grated

- When you are serving bones just make sure that they are too large to gulp down in a single bite

What do wild dogs eat? Mostly small prey animals such as mice, voles, rabbits and birds. They consume every bit of the animal, too, including the bones.

Dogs gulp their food because they can't chew and because there are no digestive enzymes in their saliva. So, you shouldn't worry about this. If you want to know more about canine digestion see Chapter 6.

A small number of dogs, maybe about one in a hundred, find the switch to raw food a little confusing and they are not quite sure what to do. Help with this, along with tips on preparing and serving their food, can be found in Chapter 5.

Variety is the spice of life

It is important that your dog receives his or her nutrition from lots of different sources. Use meat from different animals. Use different parts of the animal. Use seasonal vegetables.

Group 1: Raw, Lean Muscle Meat And Organs

Raw, lean muscle meat and organs should make up a third of your dog's daily food. You'll notice that marrowbones and knuckle ends are included in this group. Why? Because the marrow in the middle of the bone is brim full of (healthy) high-calorie fats.

SHOPPING LIST:
- Beef heart (aka ox)
- Ox tongue
- Tripe
- Lean minced or cubed chicken
- Chicken hearts
- Turkey heart
- Lamb heart
- Lean minced or cubed turkey
- Lean minced or cubed pork
- Venison meat
- Venison heart
- Lean minced or cubed duck
- Pork tongue
- Beef marrowbones – knuckle ends best
- Lean minced or cubed goat

You'll notice that I have left off two easy-to-obtain ingredients from this list: lamb mince and beef mince. The trouble with any mince is that it tends to have a high proportion of fat in it, and this is especially true of lamb and beef. If, however, you can obtain really, really lean lamb or beef it is fine to use it.

What about carcasses and wings?

Chicken, duck and turkey carcasses (aka 'backs', as in chicken backs) as well as wings can replace both the meat and the bone element of the diet depending on how meaty they are. If you can get carcasses/wings then you could feed them as often as three times a week. Unless your dog loves vegetables and will eat them without being mixed into meat, there is no need to try and feed them on the side on these days, you can just leave them out.

SHOPPING LIST:
- Chicken carcasses
- Chicken wings (remove the skin)
- Turkey carcasses
- Turkey wings (remove the skin)
- Duck carcasses (remove the skin)
- Duck wings (remove the skin)
- Whole rabbits, gutted, feet removed, beheaded and skinned
- Whole pheasant and other game

Group 2: Raw Meaty Bones

Raw, meaty bones should make up a third of your dog's daily food. I devote Chapter 7 of this book to the subject of bones, so I won't repeat everything here. The important point is that they must be raw (raw bones are surprisingly soft and dogs have such strong stomach acids they can readily digest them). In the wild up to a third of a dog's nutrition (including calcium, magnesium, complex fats and vitamins) may come from bones. Bones keep their teeth and gums clean (it has been proven that dogs with healthy teeth live longer) and exercise their upper bodies and jaws. Providing the bones are raw (cooked bones can splinter), they are 100% safe for dogs to eat.

SHOPPING LIST:
- Pork ribs
- Pork trotters
- Venison ribs
- Venison neck
- Chicken neck
- Turkey neck
- Duck neck
- Lamb ribs
- Lamb neck
- Lamb trachea
- Beef trachea

Please remember to read Chapter 7 for more on feeding raw bones.

Group 3: Raw Vegetables And Fruit

Vegetables and fruit should make up a third of your dog's daily food. It is vital that the ingredients are fresh. Tired-looking vegetables and fruit have lost most of their nutritional value. Whether you include one item from this list every day or several doesn't really matter. Unless your dog loves eating vegetables (some do), my advice is to either blend or juice the ingredients and then mix them in with the other ingredients. Vegetables and fruit are a dog's best protection against cancer.

The fruit element should never be more than a small percentage of the vegetable/fruit you serve – say no more than about 10–20%.

SHOPPING LIST:
- Broccoli
- Celery
- Celeriac*
- Chinese cabbage
- Courgette
- Beetroot*
- Carrot*
- Parsnips
- Cauliflower
- Spinach
- Kale
- Green leafy vegetables
- Butternut squash
- Pumpkin

- Pepper (red, yellow and orange but not green)
- Mangetout
- Blueberries
- Blackberries
- Raspberries
- Strawberries
- Red watermelon
- Apple*
- Pear*
- Banana (just a small piece and not too often)
- Pineapple*

* Go easy on these foods as they have a high sugar content.

Starchy vegetables to avoid: peas, potatoes, sweet potatoes, onion and leek.

Fruit to avoid: grapes, avocado and dried fruit.

Group 4: 'Boosters' Such As Eggs And Sardines

Choose ONE item from this list and add it every *other* day. In plain English: on a Monday you could add an egg, on Tuesday nothing, on Wednesday a few tinned sardines, on Thursday nothing and on Friday a teaspoon of chia seeds. These 'boosters' are not vital to the diet, but help to ensure that your dog receives a wide range of nutrients.

SHOPPING LIST:
- Eggs – *One egg for a small or medium-sized dog. Two eggs for a very large dog. Eggs are packed full of protein and valuable nutrients, essential fats and vitamins. Include shells*

- Sardines in water with no salt added – *Add one sardine for a small dog, three for a medium-sized dog and a whole tin for a large dog. Sardines are a great source of protein, trace minerals and vitamins*

- Hempseed oil – *One teaspoon. Contains valuable essential fatty acids/omegas*

- Flaxseed oil – *One teaspoon. Contains valuable omegas*

- Chia seeds – *One teaspoon. Contains valuable amino acids, fibres and minerals. Good source of omegas, too*

- Live yoghurt – *One tablespoon for every 10kg your dog weighs. Good probiotic*

Sample Menus

Just to recap: you are feeding your dog 1.5% of its body weight every day (unless there is a reason to vary this amount). The food you serve will consist of $^1/_3$ meat, $^1/_3$ meaty bone and $^1/_3$ vegetable/fruit taken from each of the groups above.

It is better not to mix sources (i.e. serve chicken with chicken). You are weighing your dog once a week and will adjust the quantities as necessary.

Below is a sample menu plan for a week. You'll notice that on a couple of days I have suggested skipping either the bone or the vegetables. The beauty of the Lucky Dog Weight Loss Plan is that you don't have to follow the rules religiously. There's a bit of flexibility.

	GROUP 1 Raw, lean muscle meat and organs	GROUP 2 Raw meaty bones	GROUP 3 Raw vegetables and fruit	GROUP 4 'Boosters' every other day
MON	Cubed pork	Pork ribs	Carrot and cauliflower	
TUE	Minced duck	Duck neck	Spinach, mange tout and banana	Sardine
WED	Beef knuckle bone	No need for extra bone	Skip for a day	
THU	Ox heart	Skip for a day	Pumpkin, celery and blueberries	Hemp-seed oil
FRI	Duck back and wings	No need for extra bone	Kale and red pepper	
SAT	Whole rabbit	No need for extra bone	Skip for a day	Live yoghurt
SUN	Minced chicken	Chicken carcass (no meat)	Cabbage, broccoli and apple	Egg

A Few Words About Treats

A treat is not food. Its purpose is either to reward a dog or, of course, to spoil them! Dogs love receiving treats and we love dispensing them. Of course, a treat is only a treat if the recipient likes it. Few dogs, for instance, consider a spinach leaf to be a treat! On the other hand, dogs (like humans) can be trained to enjoy new tastes and sensations. For example, dogs can be trained to view a piece of cut-up apple or carrot as something highly desirable. Here are a few treat tips:

• Size isn't necessarily important when it comes to treats. A tiny, tiny little piece of something desirable (for instance, a piece of cooked chicken quarter the size of a sugar lump) will be well received

• Little bits of cut-up carrot make an excellent treat. If your dog is dubious, try cooking them slightly, rubbing them on some meat or adding a few drops of real gravy to give them extra taste. Remember, carrot has a high sugar content, so go easy in terms of quantity

• Break larger treats into smaller pieces and use more sparingly

• Air-dried treats (such as air-dried liver) are high in protein but low in fat

- Avoid rawhide (high in fat) and jerky type (potentially contaminated) treats

- Apple makes a great treat. Take the same approach as you would with carrot

- Blueberries (packed full of valuable antioxidants) are easy to carry around and can also be popular

An Oscar For Oscar

Your dog may believe, and may even convince you, that he or she is starving to death from lack of food. Don't be fooled. Dogs are incredibly talented actors. In fact, because the Lucky Dog Weight Loss Plan has high quantities of protein and healthy volumes of 'good' fats your dog shouldn't actually feel hungry. A good option, when a dog is making those food eyes at you, is to distract him or her with a game or a cuddle. If you feel you simply must do something then increase the volume of fibrous vegetables in the food. Only be warned! Fibrous vegetables can have two side effects: larger volumes of, ahem, waste matter and a greater tendency to, ahem, wind.

04

EXTRA TIPS AND ADVICE

<u>04</u>

EXTRA TIPS AND ADVICE

The Lucky Dog Weight Loss Plan is, as you can see, absurdly simple and I am willing to guarantee its success if it is implemented correctly. Below are some of the little wriggles and shortcuts I have discovered since I developed the diet. There are also some facts and other information you may find interesting.

The Lucky Dog Weight Loss Plan Promotes The Right Sort Of Weight Loss

Some research done by one of the processed food manufacturers proved that a high-protein diet resulted in fat weight loss rather than muscle weight loss. If food contained 20% protein then 34% of the weight loss was muscle and 66% fat. But by increasing the protein level to 39% the muscle weight loss dropped to 14% and the fat weight loss increased to 86%.

A High-Moisture Diet Is Good For Dogs

One of the things you'll notice about the Lucky Dog Weight Loss Plan is that the food you serve will be quite moist. This is much healthier for your dog and will have the added advantage of making him or her feel fuller and less hungry. Why does moist food fill a dog up more? Think of the difference between potato crisps (high density, low moisture) and mashed potato (low density, high moisture). You have to eat a lot of crisps to feel full, but much less mashed potato. This is due to the relative moisture content.

A Word Of Warning About Kibble...

Kibble can cause special health issues. Because it is so dry (5–10% moisture compared to 70% moisture in a natural diet) and so concentrated, it fails to stimulate the dog's gastrointestinal system. Because of this, it can be dangerous to feed a dog until it feels full. Instead, one must keep the dog constantly hungry.

Exercise Made Easy

There is absolutely no doubt that exercise plays a key role in weight loss. It is possible for your dog to reach his or her target weight without increasing the amount of exercise taken, but it will slow the whole process down. Moreover, exercise brings with it huge health benefits. It will strengthen your dog's cardiovascular system and reduce his or her chances of suffering from a range of diseases. Dogs that exercise regularly are happier, too. Here are a few tips:

- Increase the amount of exercise gradually. Your dog will need to adjust to the change in regime

- If your dog is obese, take it slowly. You don't want to put extra strain on his or her joints

- If your dog has a short nose (Pugs, Pekinese, etc.), don't allow them to get out of breath as their systems can't handle strenuous exercise

- Exercise comes in many forms – be creative

- Generally, for a healthy dog, I would recommend an hour a day of vigorous exercise. It is more beneficial if the dog becomes out of breath, since this means his or her cardiovascular system is being exercised

There are dozens of different and interesting ways to exercise your dog that will make it more fun for them and you. Here are some different ideas:

- Play fetch! Use a tennis ball, Frisbee or other toy

- Treat yourself to one of those snazzy tennis ball launchers

- Join a flyball club (not suitable for obese dogs)

- Join an agility club (not suitable for obese dogs)

- Make your dog work for every treat (and be mean with the size of reward you give). For example, make him or her go up and down stairs a few times before handing over the reward

- Swimming is great exercise. There's the sea, rivers and lakes, of course, but also dedicated hydrotherapy and aquatic centres just for dogs

- Join any sort of training club. Even basic obedience training will burn up the calories

- Even getting on and off furniture or in and out of a dog bed uses up calories

Please note: It is not advisable to exercise a dog just before or after a meal.

'Look at Kong, the Eighth Wonder of the World'

This is one of my favourite lines from the 1933 movie. What does it have to do with your dog's weight-loss programme? Put a little of his or her food in a Kong (those rubber toy things with holes in them). It will take him or her hours to get the food out and in the meantime they have been provided with mental stimulation *plus* they will have used up some calories in the process. Working on a Kong is quite tiring for a dog and they are more likely to settle afterwards, rather than hanging around the kitchen in a hopeful manner. Make sure the Kong is an appropriate size for the dog. Incidentally, if you have a dog who is brilliant at getting out the food, make it a bit harder by freezing the Kong after stuffing it, and giving him or her a Kongsicle! (It is best to take it out of the freezer for 10–15 minutes before feeding to avoid freezer burn on your dog's tongue.)

Don't Let Your Dog Train You

If your dog is used to getting a food reward when they do something cute or for some other reason, remember that praise is just as effective and contains no calories!

Keep A Food Diary

A food diary is really useful because it allows you (and your vet) to understand how diet is affecting your dog's weight. All you have to do is write down what you feed your dog every day. You could also include a note about how much exercise he or she gets. Involve everyone in the family. If someone slips the dog something forbidden then please, please remember to record it. **You will find the Lucky Dog Food Diary at the back of this book.**

It Is All A Matter Of Scale(s)

Please remember to weigh your dog weekly as your dog's weight determines how much food he or she receives every day.

Think Big! Make The Food Up In Batches And Freeze It

All the food you will be serving as part of the Lucky Dog

Weight Loss Plan can be frozen. So, if you would rather not have to shop for your dog every few days, why not make larger batches of the food up, divide it into appropriately sized portions and freeze it?

When I do this, I form the food into patties (a bit like hamburger patties) and use plastic sheets to keep them separate in the freezer. You could equally well portion the food into plastic bags, containers or moulds. Incidentally, bones can be frozen as well.

Please note: There is no health risk associated with freezing food, thawing or partly thawing it, and then freezing it again. This is because modern domestic freezers are so efficient that they bring the food down to minus 18 degrees, or more – quite cold enough to stop most dangerous bacteria from forming. What does happen is that food repeatedly frozen and thawed becomes increasingly mushy and bloody.

Also, you should never thaw food in a microwave, as there is a risk that you will start to cook the bone by accident and a cooked bone should never be fed.

Water, Water, Everywhere...

Tap water can contain trace elements of all sorts of contaminants including chlorine, fluoride, arsenic, toxic pesticide residues, heavy metals and so forth. This is not good for humans and definitely not good for dogs. Filtering the water helps. You could also consider rainwater and/or artesian spring water, which tends to be the cleanest and contains the best range of valuable trace minerals.

Dogs love the taste and texture of the diet. You'll be making someone (with four paws) very happy!

The Lucky Weight Loss Plan has been approved by many vets as being safe and effective. Moreover, you can expect to see rapid results – normally within two weeks.

Please Don't Support Intensive Farming

For the most part farm animals lead short, painful lives in appalling conditions. They are kept indoors, in tiny cages, mutilated and transported hundreds and even thousands of miles before being killed. Furthermore, the way they are slaughtered is invariably drawn-out and cruel.

The photographs and imagery used by farmers, producers, food manufacturers, butchers, marketing boards and supermarkets create, by and large, entirely the wrong impression. Only a tiny percentage of farm animals lead relatively happy and natural existences.

Unless the meat you buy meets certain criteria, the chances are that it has been intensively reared. To buy it is to support cruelty to animals. Of course, it is cheaper than meat from compassionately farmed animals: having a conscience does cost a little bit extra. But if you love animals, it is money well spent. What's more, intensively reared meat is much more likely to be packed with harmful chemicals since intensively farmed animals are given many more drugs to keep them alive.

To ensure that the meat you are buying has not been intensively reared insist that:

- Chicken, pork and turkey are free range
- Rabbit and venison are free range or wild
- Lamb and beef have been grass fed or are free range

If you are buying organic meat, providing it is properly certified, you can be confident that it has been reared with animal welfare in mind.

It is much better for the environment and less wasteful to buy British. It is insane to buy lamb from, say, New Zealand when we have our own here at home. Also, beware of labelling. Ridiculous EU rules allow businesses to buy chickens in, say, Thailand but by cunning means describe them as being British. Please read the small print.

If you would like to learn more about intensive farming, you might like to contact:

• Compassion in World Farming (www.ciwf.org. uk), which was started by an ordinary British farmer

• The World Society for the Protection of Animals (www.wspa.org.uk), a leading pressure group

• The Soil Association (www.soilassociation.org), the UK's leading campaigner for higher standards of animal welfare

The Fishy Thing About Fish

Some experts suggest you incorporate fish into your dog's diet because, in the wild, wolves are, apparently, always holding their paws out to demonstrate how big their catch was and also telling stories about the one that got away.

However, there are various issues surrounding fish as an ingredient. For starters, as it were, overfishing is a massive issue and very few species are unaffected. Then there is the fact that a high percentage of fish contain heavy metals such as mercury and other poisons. In fact, raw saltwater fish often disagrees with dogs. Finally, fish farming does terrible damage to the environment.

I rarely feed fish to my own dogs and we don't sell any fish through Honey's. If you decide to make fish one of the ingredients you feed your dog, I would urge you to make sure it comes from a sustainable supply.

The Pros And Cons Of Green Tripe

If there were only one food you could feed your dog, it would have to be green tripe. Nothing else offers such a variety of digestible proteins and your dog would thrive if fed nothing else (although it would still need some raw bones, of course). What is green tripe? The dictionary defines it as: 'the entire unprocessed stomach of cud chewing animals such as cows, deer or lamb'. It has a green, fluorescent shine to it, although in colour it tends to be anything from light brown to black.

From a dog's perspective it is almost a wonder food, but from a human's perspective it has a couple of potential drawbacks.

To begin with, tripe contains a great deal of bacteria, some of which may be harmful to humans (but not dogs). For this reason, it can't be kept in the same fridge or freezer as food for human consumption. It must be handled and served carefully so that no contamination occurs. If you have any cuts or grazes on your skin you shouldn't touch it as it can lead to infection.

Then there is the smell. This is not only strong but also lingers. It's not a bad smell when you get used to it, but it's a devil to wash off and so it really is best to handle tripe using rubber gloves.

In short, it is a nuisance to deal with but well worth the effort if you can be bothered, especially as it is relatively inexpensive.

One final point: bleached tripe is worse than useless as the bleaching process strips out most of the goodness and leaves a potentially harmful chemical residue. Tripe that has been washed in plain water is not as good as green tripe but is a less bothersome alternative and 100% safe for human handling.

Reassurance About Parasites

The major dog food manufacturers clearly feel threatened by the natural feeding movement and there is definitely a campaign to discredit raw feeding. As part of this campaign, it is sometimes suggested that there are dangerous parasites in raw meat. This is incorrect.

The main reason why you don't have to be afraid of 'killer' parasites in a 'prey' animal being transferred to a 'predator' is that if this happened all predators would have become extinct long ago! Wolves simply wouldn't have survived. Also, one has to remember that, in the wild, carnivores frequently target sick and old animals as they are easier to catch and kill.

So, not only is it safe for wolves to eat raw meat, but it is safe for them to eat raw meat from poorly prey.

Another reason not to be concerned is the acidity in a wolf's (or dog's) stomach. This is so strong that few organisms can survive exposure.

The parasites that survive on a herbivore are, by and large, very different from the parasites that attack carnivores. There is one exception to this: tapeworm. These can be caught from fleas found on rabbits; so, if a dog eats a whole rabbit (as opposed to rabbit meat), there is a risk. This won't affect you, though, unless you are giving your dog whole rabbit carcasses.

Incidentally, there is a prejudice against pork, because in the distant past pigs used to carry a parasite called trichinosis. This parasite was eradicated in farmed pork in the UK (and Europe) in the 1960s. If you are still nervous about parasites (which I don't think you need to be), freeze the meat for an extended period.

A Word About Hygiene

Dogs may have stomach acids so strong that they would burn your fingers, but humans don't. Raw food does have bacteria on it that could cause health issues for humans. Keep it separate from the food you are going to eat, and thoroughly wash any surface it comes into contact with (including utensils, storage containers and so forth) as well as your hands. Use an antibacterial soap or mild disinfectant and/or wear rubber gloves. If you don't want to use harmful chemicals, vinegar is a natural alternative.

Feeding On The Move

The Lucky Dog Weight Loss Plan can pose a bit of a challenge when you are away from home. If you don't have access to a freezer, the best option is to take the food frozen and to keep it as cold as possible. It doesn't actually matter if the meat is a little smelly when served (your dog won't mind!) but after a few days the vegetable element will start to lose its nutritional value. Still, with careful management food should last for up to four or five days in a fridge.

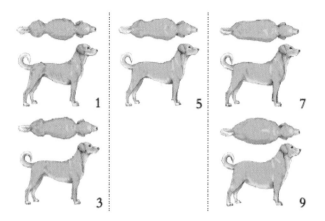

Under Ideal

1. *All bony prominences evident; no body fat. Obvious loss of muscle mass.*

3. *Ribs easily palpated. Pelvic bones becoming prominent. Obvious waist.*

Ideal

5. *Ribs palpable without excess fat covering. Waist observed behind ribs when viewed from above. Abdomen tucked up when viewed from side.*

Over Ideal

7. *Heavy fat cover; noticeable deposits over lumbar area and base of tail.*

9. *Massive fat deposits on neck and limbs. Waist and abdominal tuck absent.*

To prepare the Lucky Dog Weight Loss Plan usually takes two or three minutes, once or twice a day. Everything you need can be found in your local supermarket and/or butcher.

05

MAKING THE SWITCH TO THE LUCKY DOG WEIGHT LOSS PLAN

05

MAKING THE SWITCH TO THE LUCKY DOG WEIGHT LOSS PLAN

'At last! This is the very food I have been longing for. Thank you, thank you.' Most dogs welcome the switch to the Lucky Dog Weight Loss Plan with open paws (and open jaws!) but from time to time (I would guess, maybe, one dog in a hundred) a dog will turn its nose up and generally become sniffy at the change in diet.

Why does this happen? I have found that generally it is the really intelligent dogs from loving homes that are more likely to take a stand-offish attitude to the introduction of the Lucky Dog Weight Loss Plan. My guess is that their hunger for attention is greater than their hunger for food. Being smart, they realise that if they don't eat you'll make a fuss of them and this makes them happy. Sometimes, too, dogs become addicted to the high-carbohydrate, high-sugar, rancid-fat taste of kibble or tinned food (in the same way a child may become addicted to junk food) and they object, on principle, to the move to a healthier option.

Whatever the cause, there is no need to worry.

The most important part of the diet is raw, lean muscle meat and organs – minced, cubed or simply left as it is.

Switching Options

Be firm

A dog can go up to a week without food and be none the worse for it. Give your dog a single chance to eat every 24 hours, and if he or she doexsn't pounce on it with enthusiasm the moment you put the bowl down, lift it back up after a minute or two and wait another day. (Anyway, it is never a good idea to leave food down for your dog as snacking puts a strain on their digestive system.) Too soft-hearted for such a firm approach? Keep reading.

Mixing

Slowly start adding raw food to whatever it is you normally feed, increasing the amount every day until it is 100% raw after one or two weeks. This gives the dog's stomach time to adjust to the change. If the dog is regurgitating the food then, having checked it isn't a medical issue, extend the period over which you make the switch. It doesn't really matter if it takes a month or more.

Cooking

Take the raw food and cook it in a pan (not a microwave and not the bones). Every day cook it slightly less until it is raw. This gives the dog's stomach time to adjust to the change from sterile, processed food.

Vegetables and fruit should make up about a third of your dog's diet.
It is vital that the ingredients are fresh.

Tripe

Fast for a day and then make the switch immediately, but only feed your dog green tripe to begin with. Dogs find this incredibly easy to digest and it contains all the nutrients they need. (For more information about tripe, see Chapter 4.)

Dogs and vegetables

Some dogs love vegetables; others don't, and the ones who don't may decline to eat their food for this reason. The solution? Give in to them! Remove vegetables from their diet completely and wait for a week or two before gradually reintroducing them. Another approach is to pour a little real gravy or break an egg over the food before serving it, as this will disguise the taste.

Other Things To Watch Out For

There are other issues that you should watch out for during the switchover period.

Itchy 'hotspots'

If your dog is suffering from an 'itchy hot spot' it may be due to an intolerance to a particular protein source (such as beef). An exclusion diet (in other words a bit of trial and error) may allow you to identify the source of the issue,

Raw meaty bones should make up about a third of your dog's diet. They are packed with nutrition and also keep your dog's teeth and gums healthy.

Regurgitation immediately after eating

Regurgitation immediately after eating is almost always caused by a conditioned reflex. The dog's stomach is expecting the normal food and has prepared the wrong kind of enzymes to digest it. When the new food turns up, the system rejects it. It is quite normal in nature for a dog to eat something, vomit it up and eat it again. It is, of course, up to you whether you allow this. But you shouldn't panic. The solution to this sort of vomiting is, initially, patience and then to use one of the switching options mentioned above. Incidentally, dogs may also vomit bones because they aren't used to eating them, and some people suspect that dogs vomit a meal that they really enjoyed eating so that they can have the pleasure of eating it again! If you have been feeding the Lucky Dog Weight Loss Plan for a couple of weeks and the dog suddenly vomits, this may be an attempt to rid the body of toxins and is not unusual. Obviously, if your dog is vomiting frequently you should check with your vet that there isn't any serious underlying health problem.

Soft stools

You shouldn't panic if your dog's stools are runny. It is probably caused by the change in diet and will pass in a few days. It could also be the result of not enough bone in the diet as it is the bone that tends to make the stools firmer. The solution to runny stools is, initially, patience and then to use one of the switching options mentioned above. You could also increase the bone element of the dog's diet. If your dog seems to have a problem with a particular ingredient, try it for two or three days and then drop it and come back to it later.

A word about canine tummy upsets

There is a huge difference between soft or runny stools and diarrhoea.

It is normal, when switching diet, for dogs to experience soft or runny stools and it can occur if they aren't eating enough bone. True diarrhoea is virtually liquid – like soup. A reliable remedy (apart from increasing the amount of bone you are feeding) is to give the dog slippery elm. Some people recommend mashed boiled sweet potato (possibly with an egg) to firm up stools. If you are worried, return the dog to the old diet and start again when things have settled down. At what point do you call in a vet? In the case of runny stools don't wait more than a week. In the case of true diarrhoea you probably shouldn't delay more than 24 hours. Incidentally, true diarrhoea is not caused by raw food per se but will almost certainly be the result of either a parasite or gastrointestinal problem. If the latter, all that has happened is that the raw feeding has exposed the underlying problem.

Constipation

When some dogs are switched to a raw food diet, they can become constipated. It seems to afflict dogs who are prone to constipation the most. There are two likely reasons. First, raw food is quite moist and some dogs, not feeling as thirsty, stop drinking as much water. Second, if the bone content is even slightly too high it can cause constipation. A firm bowel movement and even a little bit of straining is normal as this is how dogs empty their anal glands. What is not normal is excessive straining, distress and no bowel movements at all. Assuming that your dog is otherwise healthy, my advice would be to reduce the bone element and to add leafy green vegetables, fruit, berries and even water to the food. It is trial and error as no two dogs will be exactly the same.

Remember that bone is a critical part of the diet and should not be removed for long periods of time. If you are worried that your dog is constipated, you should, of course, consult your vet.

06

WHY WOLVES
AND WILD DOGS
NEVER GET FAT

06

WHY WOLVES AND WILD DOGS NEVER GET FAT

So, why don't wolves and wild dogs ever get fat? In fact, why don't you ever see any fat animals in the wild, even when there is plenty of food around? There are two reasons.

First of all, and I know I have already mentioned this a couple of times so a squillion apologies for bringing it up again, every species on earth eats a biologically appropriate diet. This ensures that they receive the energy they need and can achieve optimum health.

Second, with the single exception of humans, all species self-regulate the amount of food they eat. This means that they maintain the ideal weight.

When designing the Lucky Dog Weight Loss Plan all I have done is replicate a dog's biologically appropriate diet and worked out how much food they should be eating every day.

To do this, of course, I had to study the canine digestive system. Given that I pretty much slept through biology at school, I was surprised at quite how intriguing canine digestion turned out to be. Indeed, if you love dogs I think you will find what follows fascinating.

A wolf in all but name

If you look up dogs in any encyclopaedia you will see that their Latin classification is *Canis lupus familiaris* and that they are a domesticated form of the grey wolf, aka *Canis lupus lupus*.

In other words, they are the same species.

The grey wolf has been in existence for over four million years but domesticated wolves (dogs) have only been around for some 8,000– 20,000 years.

Whether humans captured wolves and domesticated them or wolves domesticated themselves is not clear. Possibly a bit of both. What is certain is that from early on we selectively bred dogs with a view to developing certain physical and behavioural traits. Thus, over time, we created hunting dogs, retrieving dogs, guard dogs, companion dogs and so forth.

We may have managed to alter the way dogs look and, to a certain extent, think, but physiologically they haven't changed. There is absolutely no difference (apart from size) between the internal organs and digestive process of a Chihuahua and a grey wolf. This is why they should eat the same diet.

The Secrets Of Canine Digestion Revealed

The bond between humans and dogs is so close that it is easy to forget that, being different species, we have markedly different digestive systems. No species thrives on an incorrect diet and many animals become ill and die if fed inappropriately. It is possible for a species to partially adapt to a new diet: palaeontologists believe that this change takes at least 100,000 years.

Meat Glorious Meat

Dogs are carnivores. True, they can and do eat vegetable matter, but anatomically they are designed to catch, kill and eat prey. As with other predatory mammals, they have powerful muscles relative to their size, fused wrist bones and a cardiovascular system that supports both sprinting and endurance. And a quick look inside their mouth is all it takes to understand why they are really much, much closer to being carnivores than omnivores.

No matter how sweet and innocent a dog may look, the inside of his or her mouth tells a different story. Your dog's mouth is a bit like a Swiss Army knife with four main types of teeth, each designed to perform different and precise functions: catching and killing prey, tearing off meat, and grabbing, holding and crushing bones. They also work like scissors cutting sinews and muscles. None of these teeth, however, is capable of grinding food. Indeed, if you gently try to move a dog's jaw from side to side (necessary for grinding and chewing) you'll find that it is impossible. A dog's jaw can only move up and down.

All The Action Takes Place In The Stomach

A dog's digestive process starts in its stomach. This differs dramatically from humans. We use our teeth to grind our food and moisten it with saliva containing digestive enzymes so that the digestive process is well in hand by the time we swallow. Dogs, on the other hand, don't have any digestive enzymes in their saliva – there is no point because they can't grind their food, owing to having jaws that only open and close. Instead, they gulp their food with a view to getting it to where the action takes place (the stomach) as quickly as possible.

What Happens When The Food Arrives?

The stomach starts to produce digestive enzymes and other chemicals to break the food down into small molecules that can be absorbed and used by the body. Some of these enzymes are produced by the pancreas, but many are produced by other small glands in the stomach wall itself. To help the digestive process, dogs have extremely strong and corrosive stomach acids. Acidity is measured using something called pH. Neutral is pH 7, but when a dog is digesting food its stomach operates at between pH 1 and pH 2. Put in plain English: if you touched the natural acids in a dog's stomach, you would burn your fingers. Another important point in relation to this is that most enzymes are extremely sensitive to pH and won't function in the wrong environment. If a dog eats inappropriate food then its digestive system can't function properly.

Dogs Have Evolved To Eat A Lot, Quite Quickly

Dogs can consume up to 5% of their body weight in an extremely short period. To put this into perspective, it would be like a 10-stone human eating, say, seven pounds of food in a single sitting. The inside of a dog's stomach looks rather like an accordion with lots of folds. It expands when full and its muscles massage the food to ensure that the digestive juices work properly. Once all the digestible pieces of food have been dissolved, the muscles squeeze the now liquid mass into the intestine for the final stage of the process and for the absorption of the nutrients. A dog's stomach is designed to finish digesting one meal before being filled again. This process generally takes longer than for humans, although it very much depends on what the dog has eaten.

The grain problem

Why shouldn't dogs be fed grain? The answer lies in its effect on the pH balance in their stomachs. Normally, this is quite low (between pH 1 and pH 2) because only with a low pH (i.e. high acidity) can dogs digest raw meat and bones. Grain has the effect of elevating the pH level and weakening the stomach acids. Weak stomach acids mean that proper digestion becomes impossible.

This is why dogs fed a lot of grain (and there is a lot of grain in most processed dog food) produce high levels of waste matter. It goes in one end and comes out the other.

If grain is processed in some way (rolled, soaked, heated etc.) dogs can digest a small amount, which is what dog food manufacturers rely upon.

Even so, there is another issue. We humans can eat carbohydrates (such as porridge or pasta), convert them to sugars and store the energy in our bodies to use later on. Dogs have no capacity to do this. Grain (rice, wheat, corn etc.) is much cheaper than meat and easier to process, which is why so much of it is used in manufactured dog food.

What Dogs Eat In The Wild

Dogs are carnivores and the primary component of their diet is prey. This could be small animals – mice, voles, rabbits, birds, insects, and so forth – or it could be larger prey caught with the help of a pack. Either way, they eat everything – the internal organs, the meat, the bones... the lot. Dogs aren't obligate carnivores like cats. They can and do eat vegetable matter.

Wild dogs will search for rotten fruit and will eat the semi-digested contents of their prey's stomach. Some will dig up vegetables and eat grasses and herbs.

Dogs are also scavengers. They eat the leftovers from every animal that is killed or has died. As Ian Billinghurst, a leading proponent of natural feeding, has pointed out, dogs receive 'valuable nutrients from materials that we humans find totally repugnant. Things like vomit, faeces and decaying flesh'. With regard to the faeces, incidentally, these contain the dead and living bodies of millions upon billions of bacteria. They are an excellent source of protein, essential fatty acids, fat-soluble vitamins, minerals, antioxidants, enzymes and fibre.

Not wanting to dwell on an unpleasant subject, but if you have a dog that is on a processed food diet he or she may be eating faeces in order to try to stay healthy (although if a dog is eating canine or feline faeces it will probably be because they contain the undigested flavourings used to make their processed food palatable).

What Dogs Don't Eat In The Wild

Almost as important as what dogs eat in the wild is what they don't eat.

For starters, they don't necessarily eat every day. Depending on where they live, the season, the size of the pack, the available prey and other factors, they may eat as infrequently as every second or third day or even longer without suffering any ill effects. A healthy dog can go a week without food.

Second, and perhaps more important, they don't eat 'complete' meals. Dogs meet their nutritional requirements over time. They will eat what they need or seek it out if their body is telling them they need it.

This is referred to as the 'balance over time concept'. It is crucial to the way dogs should be fed because there is evidence that dogs fed all the ingredients they need in proportion at every meal suffer increased health problems.

Finally, dogs don't eat grain. They can't digest it properly and, even if they could, they can't convert it into sugar and store it for later use.

Reduce your vet bills by up to 85%!

Mogens Eliasen, in his book *Raw Food for Dogs*, quotes a major Australian study on natural feeding. He points out that 'dogs fed on a natural diet develop a strong immune system that will cause your vet bills to go down, maybe even dramatically'. He goes on to remark that the kennels which switched from feeding kibble to raw food 'experienced a significant reduction in their vet bills' with the average saving being 85%! In other words, where they were spending £100 before, they now only spend £15. As explained in Chapter 8, dogs on a natural diet have also been shown to live on average a third longer.

Most dogs are deliriously happy when you serve them raw food for the first time but a few find the new diet a little puzzling and need some help switching.

07

GIVE A DOG A BONE

07

GIVE A DOG A BONE

You can't have failed to notice that an important constituent ingredient in the Lucky Dog Weight Loss Plan is raw bone. Let me explain.

In The Wild, Dogs Eat Their Prey, Bones And All

In the wild, providing they have a choice, all animals eat what is best for them. For dogs this means small prey or, if hunting in a pack, a share of larger prey. They are thrifty, too. Nothing is wasted and that includes the bones. Initially, these are ripped, torn, chewed and sucked to remove all the meat and marrow. Then they are gnawed, crunched and (if small enough) eaten whole.

There has been some fantastically interesting (if gory) research in Australia proving this, in which scientists studied the insides of hundreds of wild dogs (don't even ask). In studies by S. J. O. Whitehouse (*Australian Wildlife Research* magazine, 1977, 4(2): 145–50) and A. E. Newsome (*Australian Wildlife Research* magazine, 1983, 10(3): 477–86), hundreds of dogs were examined across a wide geographical area. The results were conclusive not only on the bone issue, by the way, but also on other dietary preferences. No wild dog, for example, ever eats grain.

(Please note: There is more research available on the

same topic, including detailed studies by Neville Buck, who studied a wide range of dogs and wolves at Howletts and Port Lympne Wild Animal Parks in the UK.)

Bones Are Packed Full Of Vital Nutrients

It is easy to understand why the dog wants the meat and marrow, but what makes the bone itself so desirable? The answer is that bones contain a huge number of nutrients that are vital to your dog's health. These include:

- Minerals, including calcium, magnesium and phosphorous

- Protein-containing essential amino acids, including lysinet

- Essential fatty acids

- Fat-soluble vitamins (A, D and E)

- Blood-forming nutrients (these are in the marrow), including copper and iron

Bones Keep Your Dog's Teeth And Gums Healthy

Meaty bones are nature's toothbrushes. They keep your

dog's teeth clean and gums healthy. Plaque can't build up and decay is prevented. As a result your dog shouldn't develop any of the nasty oral diseases to which many of those on processed food are prone. It will also mean he or she has sweeter breath.

You may be interested to know that a growing number of vets believe that there is a close connection between oral health and general health. One veterinary dentist who has studied this is Dr Gary Beard, who is based at Auburn University in Alabama. In 1991, he wrote a paper pointing out that heart failure, hepatic compromise, renal failure and other serious diseases in dogs could be a direct result of poor oral hygiene. The same year another US vet, Dr Richard Hamlin, of Ohio State University, proposed that diseases of the heart, liver and lungs could be caused this way.

Bones Provide Great Exercise, And Help With Mental Health

Two further benefits of giving your dog bones should be mentioned:

1. They provide your dog with exercise, strengthening their jaws and upper body

2. They keep your dog occupied. Dogs that have a bone to chew are happier and calmer

A word about marrowbones. Dogs love marrowbones – the marrow being the creamy centre in the middle of the bone. The upside of marrow is that it is high in nutritional value; the downside is that it is high in fat. If you are feeding a dog that is trying to lose weight, then either scoop some or all of the marrow out or choose another type of bone.

Some Bone Feeding Tips

• Dogs love bones from pretty much any animal or bird you care to mention

• A good bone to start with is a beef marrowbone. Ask the butcher to cut it to the right size for your dog: too large to be swallowed in a single gulp, small enough to handle

• In terms of size the general rule is that a chewing bone should be longer than the width of the dog's mouth

• Carcasses (yes, carcasses!) from chickens, turkeys and ducks are excellent, too

• Only feed raw bones. When a bone is cooked, it hardens and may splinter

• Choose bones from young animals. Most bones bought from a butcher will be from a younger animal, but it is worth checking. Older animals (and birds) may have harder bones, again more likely to splinter

• The first time you give your dog a raw bone, stay around to watch. Inexperienced dogs can become overexcited and there is a slim possibility of choking. For this reason a large, meaty knucklebone is perfect. Lamb bones and especially ribs, although excellent (if fattening), can get caught in the mouth and should only be fed to more experienced dogs. Also, hooves are not a good idea as they can splinter. If your dog always chews all the meat off first, then lamb necks need to be treated with caution

• If your dog is new to the raw food diet, I recommend limiting the amount of 'bone chewing' time to begin with. You could start with half an hour a day and build from that

Please note: There are a few instances where bones should be fed with caution or not at all. If a dog has just had stomach or anal gland surgery, you should give bones a miss during convalescence and until the wounds have healed. Some dogs just can't get on with whole or large chewing bones, in which case simply stick to feeding a ground bone as part of the diet.

Your dog's mouth is like a Swiss Army knife with teeth that can grab, stab, hold, cut, saw, tear, scrape, break and crush. Carnivore's teeth!

This is a wolf. Humans have bred dogs for certain looks and behaviour traits but they remain so closely related to wolves that they can interbreed.

Dogs can't digest grain. That's why you never see a dog stalking a wheat field. They are rotten cooks, too. That's why they eat all their food raw.

08

THE UNPALATABLE TRUTH ABOUT MODERN DOG FOOD

08

THE UNPALATABLE TRUTH ABOUT MODERN DOG FOOD

Low in protein, high in carbohydrates and drenched in rancid fat, modern dog food is the primary cause of canine weight gain. True, some dogs don't take enough exercise and others are given rather more treats than is perhaps good for them, but the real problem is their diet. In a nutshell (often used as an ingredient, as it happens), modern, processed dog food is having a disastrous effect on our woofers' waistlines.

Of course, if the television commercials, advertisements and labelling are to be believed, modern dog food is the only safe thing to give a dog. It contains nothing but natural goodness, has been scientifically formulated and is endorsed by experts, including vets. What's more, if your dog is suffering from any particular ailment (including being overweight or obese) there is almost certainly a food designed to put it right. Pet food manufacturers would have it that they are your dog's best friend. Once you learn the truth, you may begin to feel otherwise. Indeed, you may conclude that you have been misled and deceived.

From bad to worse: special diet food

The same dog manufacturers that are helping to cause weight issues in dogs have the audacity to sell special diet food. The diet food is not, on the whole, so different from the normal food they sell with one definite exception. It frequently contains a sizeable percentage of crude fibre. Crude fibre consists of ingredients that have little or no nutritional value for a dog. It helps to make a dog feel full, albeit temporarily, and has the added advantage (from the manufacturers' perspective) of being extremely inexpensive. Crude fibre goes in one end of a dog and comes out the other!

The Law Doesn't Protect Dogs

There is a considerable volume of British and European legislation controlling the manufacture of dog food but it barely considers the health of the animals eating it. Its real purpose is to protect the human food chain. This quote (the italics are mine), taken from the guidance given to pet food manufacturers, demonstrates how little the government cares:

> • For pets, the main part of the risk assessment when setting the maximum permitted levels for *undesirable substances* will generally be the extent to which the animal can tolerate them

In other words, it is legal to use *undesirable substances* in dog food providing they don't kill the animal immediately.

Another disturbing quote from the same guide refers to ingredients (my italics):

> • The material of animal origin used by the pet food industry comprises those parts of animals which are either deemed surplus to human consumption or are not normally consumed by people in the UK, and derived from animals inspected and passed as fit for human consumption *prior to slaughter*. Animal material of this nature, which is not intended for human consumption, is classified as *animal by-products* under the EC Regulation

This innocuous statement allows manufacturers to make their food from so-called *by-products*, that is to say hooves, tails, testicles, ears and other bits of animal. It also authorises them to use ingredients that are not suitable for human consumption. How so? If the *by-products* or meat come from an animal that was fit for human consumption *prior to slaughter*, that's fine. The meat could be a year old and completely rotten for all the legislators care.

The notes about labelling are also revealing:

> • The labelling requirements for pet food are less onerous than those for feed for farmed livestock [for humans]. For livestock, the ingredients must be declared individually in descending order by weight, but pet food manufacturers have the option to declare them by category – e.g., 'meat and animal derivatives', 'oils and fats', 'cereals', 'vegetable protein extracts'

The significance of this is huge, as it allows manufacturers to hide the actual ingredients being used in their dog food.

What are animal by-products and derivatives?

The term 'animal by-products' refers to heads, hooves, feet, viscera and other animal parts you may prefer not to think about. The term 'animal derivatives' refers to hearts, lungs, muscle meat, testicles, and so forth.

Manufacturers can claim food is 'organic' and even 'fit

for human consumption' but that doesn't mean that the ingredients are of high quality. A lung from an organic cow falls into both these categories but you wouldn't necessarily want to eat it.

Watch out for 'palatability enhancers'

The leading raw food expert, Mogens Eliasen, warns against another rarely discussed ingredient in processed food – palatability enhancers:

• Manufacturing of these chemicals is a whole industry on its own, supporting the pet food manufacturers with drugs that both taste good and make the animal addicted to the food, once it gets a taste of it. It is literally no different than giving a teenager cocaine or heroin in order to create a customer for more drugs

A concise history of dog food

One way to understand the dog food industry is to study its history.

Modern dog food was invented by James Spratt, an American living in England, who launched the first complete dog food – a biscuit made of wheat meal, vegetables and blood – in 1860. Almost immediately mill owners saw its potential as a way of selling their by-products (basically floor sweepings) and low-cost meat meal at a much higher price than they would otherwise achieve.

From day one, dog food producers made extravagant claims for their products and paid vets for endorsements. Interestingly, the basic recipe for dried dog food, manufacturers' claims and the marketing methods they use have barely changed at all in over 150 years.

Ken-L-Ration, the first canned dog food, was launched after the First World War, when over supply led to horsemeat becoming almost worthless. Demand grew and by the end of the 1960s all but a tiny percentage of dogs living in developed nations came to be fed on manufactured dog food. Perhaps this isn't surprising when one thinks how consumers moved from old-fashioned cooking to modern convenience foods.

A Licence To Print Money

It isn't just that the legislation doesn't consider canine health; it is entirely skewed in the manufacturers' favour. As you can see from the quotes above, they can put in almost any ingredient they want (providing it doesn't actually poison the dog) and can be misleading in what they tell consumers. How did this happen? Since the industry came into being, manufacturers have managed to persuade both the public and legislators that they are experts and can be trusted. They have used clever marketing techniques and veterinary endorsements to great effect and have been much aided by consumer demand for convenience.

It also helps that for many years the industry has been dominated by five multinational corporations, which between them control around 80% of the worldwide market. They are Nestlé (Purina, Bakers etc.), Del Monte (the Heinz range of pet foods), MasterFoods/Mars (Royal Canin, Pedigree, etc.), Procter & Gamble (Iams, Eukanuba etc.) and Colgate-Palmolive (Hill's Science Diet, Nature's Best etc.).

These companies lobby hard to ensure that their business interests aren't disturbed by unhelpful legislation. Their biggest single market is the USA, where pet food accounts for $15 billion a year. But the UK market is still sizeable with over £1 billion a year spent on dog food alone.

It isn't just the overall size of the market that makes it so attractive to manufacturers. Processed dog food is incredibly profitable. As one commentator pointed out:

• What most consumers don't realise is that the pet food industry is an extension of the human food and agriculture industries. Pet food provides a convenient way for slaughterhouse offal, grains considered unfit for human consumption and similar waste products to be turned into profit

Why Modern, Processed Dog Food Is So Bad

It contains low-quality ingredients

Modern, processed dog food is generally made using extremely low-quality ingredients. As explained elsewhere in this chapter, that means animal by-products and derivatives and low-quality grain. To offer just one example, chicken protein could, in reality, consist of chicken feathers.

It has been cooked

Modern, processed dog food has been cooked. Cooking alters the food's chemical structure, destroys much of its nutritional value and makes it extremely difficult for a dog to digest. A processed food diet, because it is cooked, forces the pancreas to work harder and to draw other enzymes from the bloodstream. This can leave a dog physically vulnerable because the enzymes in the blood are supposed to be protecting the body, not aiding digestion. A number of medical studies show that the pancreas enlarges on a diet of processed food. An enlarged organ means excessive function. Excessive function can lead to degeneration. It is a similar story when it comes to amino acids. Cooking at high temperatures alters the arrangement of these acids, making half of them unusable by the canine body.

It contains grain

Grain is used a great deal in modern, processed dog food as it is inexpensive and gives it bulk. Some food will contain up to 65% grain, although this may not be apparent from the labelling. In the wild, less than 1% of a dog's diet will be grain(see Chapter 6 for more detail).

Food that is advertised as being 'grain-free' may be even worse than food with grain in it. Why? As mentioned earlier, it may be free from grain, but it won't be free of carbohydrates. If you look at the package label, you'll see potato, sweet potato, lentils, peas (pea starch), chickpeas, tapioca or another carbohydrate source(s). Carbohydrates can lead to blood sugar fluctuations, insulin resistance, obesity, diabetes and other health problems in dogs.

It contains fibre

Modern, processed dog food contains a high percentage of fibre, described as 'crude fibre' because it is of such low quality. In most cases the fibre takes the form of peanut hulls, almond shells, empty grain hulls, beet pulp and so forth. None of these things offers any nutritional value to dogs.

It contains preservatives

Chemical preservatives are added to keep the food from going off. Where there are no added preservatives, it is either because the food has been heated to such a high temperature that no preservatives are necessary or because the original ingredients already contained sufficient preservatives.

It contains artificial colouring

Dried and canned food is usually grey. For this reason food colouring is added to give it a more natural appearance. Many trainers believe that the artificial colouring is one of the causes of behavioural issues in dogs.

It contains binders

In the manufacturing process many of the ingredients in dog food are rendered, that is to say they are heated until they turn into a liquid. In order to make it look like kibble or 'chunks of meat' chemical binders are added.

It contains unhealthy fats

Many commercial dog foods have fat sprayed on them as a way of making them palatable. Fat may also be added to improve nutritional value. The quality of this fat is usually poor. Fat can be recycled from deep-fat fryers in restaurants and tallow that rises from rendering plants. It may be rancid.

Dogs receive a third of their nutrition from bones and, thanks to the strength of their stomach acids, have no trouble digesting them.

Bones are nature's toothbrush. They keep your dog's teeth and gums healthy.

Having a bone to chew will keep your dog from getting bored and will also help to strengthen his or her jaws and upper body. It's like a mini-workout.

Up To Nine Out Of Ten Canine Health Issues May Be Caused By Diet

A growing number of vets and nutritionists believe that many if not most of the medical conditions that dogs are being treated for nowadays are a direct result of their diet. Tom Farrington, Honey's Chief Veterinary Surgeon, considers that as many as nine out of ten canine health issues – everything from relatively minor problems such as bad breath, flatulence, itchiness, allergies and dry skin through to major problems such as cancer, liver disease, heart disease and kidney disease – may be directly related to processed food. As Ian Billinghurst, author of *Give Your Dog a Bone*, says:

  • Our dogs' disease problems are increasing on a par with their increasing consumption of processed and cooked foods. . . dog food manufacturers take useless waste from the human food industry and sell it as dog food. Why do they bother? Advertising implies that they are there to promote the health of dogs. Their primary concern is in fact profit. The laws which govern dog food production do not require it to promote health, reproduction, growth or longevity.

If one cares about dogs it is very easy to get worked up about the processed dog food industry. It is a scandal waiting to happen. The only difference between this situation and what occurred with tobacco, asbestos, powdered milk formula, fast food and all the other consumer campaigns that have led to major changes is that the victims of the processed dog food industry can't speak for themselves.

Dogs On A Raw-Food Diet Live Longer

An Australian study (quoted by Mogens Eliasen) demonstrated that a dog's life expectancy increased by 30% when they were fed a raw, natural diet. Dogs that normally were expected to live until age 12 maintained a healthy life until they were 16 years old. This rather implies that dogs fed a processed food diet are leading shorter lives, which, in turn, prompts the question: how long can manufacturers of harmful processed food get away with their lies?

09

A CHAPTER ABOUT
SOMETHING NO ONE
LIKES TO MENTION

09

A CHAPTER ABOUT SOMETHING NO ONE LIKES TO MENTION

There's no point in beating about the bush: this chapter is about your dog's poo. Why? Because it is an important indicator of your dog's health.

Before we begin, some good news. Dogs on a raw food diet produce much less excrement, and what little there is of it biodegrades quickly and doesn't smell.

Normal? What's Normal?

A normal stool should be soft, yet firm. Its colour will be determined by the dog's diet: anything from a mid-brown to nearly black is usual. The more meat in the diet, the softer and darker it tends to be.

It is normal to find a greyish bag of slime around your dog's stool from time to time. This is the old mucous membrane, which the intestine sheds every few months.

It is also normal to see the remains of vegetables in the stool. This is vegetable matter the dog hasn't digested and it helps to stimulate the mechanical function of the intestine.

A Reason To Be Firm

It is important that your dog passes relatively firm (even quite hard) stools on a regular basis. Why? In the area under the tail, dogs have two anal glands. These excrete a particular smell when dogs move their bowels, thus allowing them to mark territory.

Dog faeces are normally firm, and the anal glands usually empty when the dog defecates, lubricating the anal opening in the process. When the dog's stools are soft, they may not exert enough pressure on the glands, which may then fail to empty. This may cause discomfort as the full anal gland pushes on the anus. If you see a dog pulling its bottom along the floor, it could well be because its anal glands are causing it a problem.

If you want to firm your dog's stools up, the simplest way is to add bone.

Stool Guide

• Very dark or black. This is caused by a high percentage of meat in the diet, especially liver and other offal

• Greyish. Usually the result of eating grain and/ or processed food

• Light-coloured, especially greyish. May be caused by a liver or pancreatic problem, so consult your vet

- Greasy stool. When dogs have a pancreatic problem, they are unable to digest fat efficiently. A greasy, sour-smelling stool may be an indication of an underlying pancreatic issue. Discuss with your vet

- Foamy stool. Could be an infection in the intestine or colon as a result of undigested fat. Again, you should probably discuss with your vet

- Very hard stool. If your dog is on a processed food diet then the cause is probably one of the ingredients included to keep the stools firm: it is not unknown for dog food companies to use sawdust for this purpose! If your dog is on a raw food diet, a hard stool is usually the result of a healthy meal of bone

- Blood in the stool. This may be caused by anything from a parasite (such as a worm) to a stool that is too firm. You should keep a sample (sorry!) to show to your vet. Bear in mind that the blood may not be red. If it is not fresh, it may appear almost black

- Soft and runny stools. A soft, runny or watery stool is not necessarily anything to worry about unless it lasts for several days or is combined with other symptoms (such as blood in the stool or vomiting). It is normal for stools to be soft, runny or watery when a dog changes diet or eats something that it doesn't want to digest

Processed dog food may result in as many as nine out of ten visits to the vet.

THE LUCKY DOG WEIGHT LOSS PLAN

BENBOW'S DOG MIXTURE

TRADE   **MARK**

REGISTERED

INFALLIBLE FOR PRODUCING FIRST-RATE CONDITION IN

GREYHOUNDS

Testimonials received from Owners
and Trainers of

X   **45**   X

WATERLOO CUP WINNERS

Sold in bottles and capsules.   Of all Chemists and Druggists everywhere, or from—

BENBOW'S DOG MIXTURE CO., 2, Bartholomew Close, E.C.1

The recipe for processed dog food hasn't changed much in 160 years: render dirt-cheap ingredients unsuitable for human consumption, add artificial colouring etc., and pay a vet to endorse it.

Processed pet food manufacturers make some deeply suspect claims.

Why Raw Food Produces So Much Less Waste

Mogens Eliasen, a raw feeding expert, has published information about the volume of stools compared to the volume of food being eaten. Meat, offal and animal fat are almost completely digested. The amount of excrement produced will represent between 2 and 7% of the food being eaten. Fruit and vegetables produce around 30–60% waste. Kibble, on the other hand, produces 60–80% waste. This is because dogs are able to take a great deal of nutrition from meat, organs and animal fat but not from processed food.

When To Be Worried About Diarrhoea

If your dog has true diarrhoea for 24 hours or soft stools for more than three days, or if it has diarrhoea one day, normal stools for a few days, and then diarrhoea again until it ends up mostly having diarrhoea, then there may be an underlying health issue and you should consult your vet.

If your dog has diarrhoea together with another symptom, such as blood in the stool, vomiting, fever or a change in behaviour, then you should consult your vet.

Good News For Your Garden

Dogs on the Lucky Dog Weight Loss Plan, that is to say

naturally fed dogs, produce less excrement and what they produce breaks down quickly. As it has no harmful chemicals in it, it won't damage your lawn. If you feed your dog raw food there will be fewer chemicals in its urine, too. This will mean that the urine is less likely to damage your grass or turn it yellow.

10

MYTH BUSTER!

10

MYTH BUSTER!

Because the Lucky Dog Weight Loss Plan involves feeding your dog raw meat and raw bones you may find that some people try to dissuade you from introducing it to your dog.

The arguments you'll hear against raw feeding can be very convincing, especially if supported by vets and other experts.

Below, I look at the most common myths and explain why they don't stack up.

Myth One: Dogs Aren't Wolves

One of the main reasons why natural feeding makes such sense is that dogs and wolves are the same species, the only difference being that dogs have been domesticated.

It is sometimes suggested that because dogs have been domesticated their physiology and digestive systems have evolved and no longer resemble those of the wolf. Therefore, the argument goes, the idea that they should eat the same diet as wolves (or wild dogs) is wrong.

This line of reasoning falls apart both in the bedroom and on the dissecting table! Wolves and dogs can interbreed. The digestive system of a Chihuahua and the digestive system of a wolf are identical in everything but scale. Yes, dogs may have been eating a certain amount of cooked food for the last 8,000–20,000 years but (a) it has only been a percentage of their diet, (b) it is has only been a percentage of domesticated dogs and (c) it hasn't been long enough for them to change the way their bodies digest and absorb nutrients.

The idea (sometimes suggested) that dogs have adapted to processed food since it was invented in 1860 is laughable. It is possible for species to partially adapt to a new diet but palaeontologists believe that it takes at least 100,000 years and probably a great deal longer.

Myth Two: Raw Food Is Home To (Dangerous) Salmonella

You can pretty much ignore anything anyone says to you about the dangers of salmonella poisoning in relation to raw feeding.

Salmonella poses a very, very low risk to humans and an even lower risk to dogs. It is present in 80–85% of all raw chicken and yet the number of people who actually suffer from salmonella poisoning is tiny. It is even rarer for a dog to suffer from it and it is interesting to note that when tests were done and dogs were fed infected meat only one-third had any evidence at all of salmonella in their faeces. In other words, the canine stomach acids (which are strong enough to burn your fingers) killed the vast majority of it off.

So, what is salmonella? Salmonella is a bacterium that can cause some unpleasant reactions in our gastrointestinal system, like vomiting and diarrhoea, and often fever. The attack may last about a week. There was some interesting research done in the US which showed that people have a risk of about 0.25% per year of getting infected with salmonella, and 0.05 ppm (ppm = 'parts per million') of dying of a salmonella infection. To put this in perspective, this compares to a yearly risk of 108 ppm for a man (33 ppm for a woman) of getting murdered, about 100 ppm for getting killed in a car accident and 11 ppm for a person less than 91 years old dying of influenza or pneumonia.

What chance is there of a human catching it from a dog? Dogs do not carry salmonella in their saliva or on their skin, not even after eating 100% salmonella-infected raw food. But, when they do eat salmonella-infected food, about one-third of them will show a moderate concentration of salmonella in their faeces – yet no clinical signs of being sick. The only way a human can catch salmonella from a dog is by, to put it bluntly, eating its you-know-what!

Incidentally, dogs eating a processed food diet are just as likely to have salmonella in their system, as it is easy to pick up in parks and elsewhere.

Human beings have been made paranoid about bacteria. In fact, there are more bacteria on a shopping trolley handle than on a piece of raw chicken.

Myth Three: Raw Food Contains Dangerous Parasites

In the wild, dogs will usually go for the easiest prey, often animals that are frail and sick. They also eat meat that is rotten, meat that has been buried for weeks and then dug up and, of course, meat that contains parasites. In all these instances they suffer no, or very few, ill effects.

Nevertheless, it is sometimes argued that raw feeding is dangerous to canine and human health because the meat may contain parasites.

This is incorrect for two reasons. First, the food-borne parasites to which dogs are vulnerable do not pose any risk to humans. Second, a dog's stomach acids are so strong that they destroy almost all known food-borne parasites likely to be of harm to them.

If you are still worried about parasites (which I don't think you need to be), freeze the food first for an extended period of time. This will deal with all but a very few, very rare parasites that are never found in food suitable for human consumption.

Myth Four: Raw-Fed Dogs Are At Risk From Neospora

Neospora is a very interesting issue, especially as it was only discovered relatively recently. There have been lots of studies on its effect in cattle but there is almost no research in relation to dogs. Neospora is a parasite and, so far, it seems to be very prevalent in beef herds: up to 80% of them are infected.

Can it be transmitted from cattle to dogs via meat? If it can, what effect does it have on the dog? Finally, is there any risk to humans? There have been so few cases reported in dogs that there is almost nothing to go on. The dogs that seem most at risk are puppies and dogs with compromised immune systems. It seems to follow the same model as toxoplasmosis and coccidiosis. But there are no properly documented cases of it affecting raw-fed dogs. Amongst pro-raw feeding vets, the basic feeling is that if it were a serious risk we would be hearing a lot more about it.

There is no need to worry about this risk, especially as neospora has probably been present in dogs and cattle for hundreds of thousands of years.

Myth Five: Raw-Fed Dogs Are At Risk Of Renal Failure

It has been suggested that feeding a dog bones puts it at risk of renal failure, owing to the high amount of calcium and phosphorus to be found in a natural diet.

Calcium is vital to your dog's health and is the most common mineral in the body. The majority of it (99%) is in the bones, with the rest distributed between other tissues and blood. Calcium has an indispensable role in major bodily functions. It is required for the transmission of nerve impulses. It is required for muscle contraction. It is a vital component in the blood-clotting mechanism. It is the structural component of bones and, hence, is of vital importance in growing animals.

Phosphorus is the other dietary mineral required in a relatively high amount. About 80% of phosphorus in the body is found in bones and teeth, principally as apatite salts and as calcium phosphate. It is located in every cell of the body. Phosphorus is also intimately involved in the acid base buffer system of blood and other bodily fluids, as a component of cell walls and cell contents as well as phospholipids, phospho-proteins and nucleic acids.

Chronic signs of deficiency include rickets in young animals and osteomalacia (softening of the bones) in adults, poor growth and lactation performance, and unsatisfactory fertility. Phosphorus is required at levels slightly less than calcium. Meat or organ meats are relatively high in phosphorus but relatively low in calcium.

It is completely wrong to say that raw feeding – eating bones and meat – causes renal failure! To begin with, in a well-balanced raw food diet calcium and phosphorus will be in the correct proportions. Then there is the fact that raw food has lower levels of phosphorus than most canned or dried food. The idea that a high-protein diet increases the chance of renal failure has been pretty much blown out of the water as rubbish.

Myth Six: Raw-Fed Dogs Are At Risk Of Choking On Bones

Bones, it is suggested, can cause dogs to choke or may rupture the stomach or intestine. In fact, dogs are more than capable of digesting raw, uncooked bones. This is thanks to their strong stomach acids. They are much more likely to choke on dried, processed food, which usually has a water content of between 5 and 10%, far below the 70% water content of a natural diet.

Myth Seven: Raw Food Is Covered In Bacteria

Yes, it is! But dogs are surprisingly well equipped to deal with bacteria. Their saliva contains lysozyme, an enzyme that destroys harmful bacteria. Their short digestive tract is designed to push through food and bacteria quickly without giving bacteria time to colonise. The extremely acidic environment in the gut is also a good bacteria colonisation deterrent.

Incidentally, processed dog food is as much of a risk in terms of bacteria: 'Pet foods, commercial or homemade, provide an ideal environment for bacterial proliferation' (LeJeune, J. T. and D. D. Hancock, 2001, 'Public health concerns associated with feeding raw meat diets to dogs' *Journal of the American Veterinary Medical Association* 219(9): 1224). The starches, rancid fats and sugars in kibbled foods provide much better food sources for bacteria than the proteins in raw meat do.

11

**HOW TO MAINTAIN A
HEALTHY WEIGHT**

11

HOW TO MAINTAIN A HEALTHY WEIGHT

The Lucky Dog Weight Loss Plan is the single most effective way I have found to help overweight and obese dogs lose those unwanted pounds (or, if you have a metric dog on your paws, kilograms).

Once your dog has reached his or her target weight, what should you do?

Obviously you don't want to return to the food that caused the problem in the first place. Instead, my strong recommendation is to stick with the Lucky Dog Weight Loss Plan but to make a few small adjustments, as described below.

Don't Rush It

My suggestion is that you allow your dog to get a little thinner than you feel he or she should be. Not much, just enough to give you a bit of wriggle room, as it were.

Don't rush to change the choice of ingredients or the volume you serve, either. Rather, you should gradually make the changes I propose below.

Consider Different Ingredients

While you have been turning your dog into a new, thinner, altogether happier hound such delicacies as minced beef, lamb and chicken skin will have been off the menu because they all contain higher levels of fat.

Once your dog has reached his or her target weight you can slowly start to introduce a wider range of ingredients, such as:

- minced beef
- minced lamb
- chicken wings with the skin on
- turkey wings with the skin on

Switch To 'Maintenance' Portions

You have been giving your dog slightly less food than he or she needs, which is why his or her weight has been dropping.

Now you can start to feed very slightly more.

You'll find, after a while, that you can adjust the portion size entirely by feel and without reference to the bathroom scales. Indeed, lots of successful raw feeders simply watch their dogs carefully and adjust the quantity as they go.

There is no hard-and-fast rule but for a dog weighing 11kg and over, roughly 2% of their body weight in food (including edible bones) every day should be about right

Dog food manufacturers have spent the last 160 years trying to persuade people that processed food is as good as a natural diet. Don't listen to them.

for a maintenance diet. In other words, a 20kg dog should be eating roughly 400g.

If you have a working dog, an underweight dog or a dog that exercises a great deal, then up this amount to between 2 and 5% of body weight per day.

If you have an elderly or overweight dog then reduce the amount to between 1% and 2% of body weight per day.

You can serve the food in as many meals as you want and at whatever time, but it should never be left down for the dog to eat when he or she feels like it.

For dogs under 11kg in weight try:
- 1–2kg: 10% of body weight
- 3–4kg: 7% of body weight
- 5–8kg: 5% of body weight
- 9–10kg: 3% of body weight
- 11kg+: 2% of body weight

If you would like more detailed advice please get in touch with Honey's (see Chapter 14 for contact information). These percentages are for guidance only.

You might also be interested to know that because wolves exercise so much they need about three times as much food as a typical dog.

Why Fasting Is Good For Your Dog's Health

From start to finish it can take a dog anything up to 20 hours to digest a full meal, a full meal being the amount it

Ironically, a bowl of kibble (due to the starches, rancid fats and sugars it contains) is more likely to host salmonella and other harmful bacteria than a bowl of raw food.

can fit in its stomach at a single sitting. This is a very long time when compared to humans, who eat much smaller meals and digest them much faster. Why is the time it takes a dog to digest important? Because a dog's digestive system needs to rest for periods to operate at optimum efficiency. More than this, if the system doesn't get a chance to rest it can be harmful to the dog's health (it needs the time for its liver to transform fat to glucose). My advice is to feed your dog once a day, never to leave food down for it ('eat it or lose it' being the rule) and to fast your dog at least once a week.

Achieving Balance

Just to remind you, dogs don't eat completely balanced meals in the wild, but get the nutrition they need over time. You don't, therefore, have to worry too much about balancing each meal you feed. Rather, you should be thinking about the balance over a week or even a month.

What To Say To Your Butcher

It is definitely worth finding a good butcher as it will save you a great deal of time and money. Also, if you live anywhere near a slaughterhouse, see if they can supply you. Either way, it is much, much easier if you have plenty of freezer space.

When searching for a butcher, explain what you are doing and ask for:

- Scraps
- Mince (this should be 'visually lean')
- Inexpensive cuts
- Offal (heart, kidneys and liver)
- Raw, meaty bones
- Chicken, turkey, duck, pheasant and other carcasses

With regard to the scraps and the mince, it is fine for it to have some fat in it, but it shouldn't be too fatty (more than 15% fat would be a problem). So far as inexpensive cuts are concerned, every butcher has his own ideas what these might be. Take 'skirt', which is the diaphragm under the ribs. Some butchers sell this for next to nothing; others know that there is good, lean meat to be had there and charge quite a bit for it. An efficient butcher will find you inexpensive ways to feed your dog.

Some people feel it is important that the meat they buy for their dogs is suitable for human consumption. Others don't. The truth is that the dogs are unlikely to mind if it is a bit smelly and you shouldn't be too obsessed with the 'best before' date.

Honey's

If you are looking for a convenient supply of ethically sourced meat and bones, try Honey's Real Dog Food.

Opposite: Benefits of a raw food diet include a glossy coat, healthy skin, lean muscle tone, robust immune system, sweet-smelling breath, healthy teeth and gums, increased energy, better digestion and a strong heart.

12

**SAFE WEIGHT LOSS
FOR POORLY DOGS**

12

SAFE WEIGHT LOSS FOR POORLY DOGS

This chapter is about achieving safe weight loss for dogs that have other health conditions.

The first and most important point I want to make is that you shouldn't start your dog on a weight loss plan involving a change of diet and/or more exercise without consulting your vet.

To help you decide on your best course of action, I have pulled together my various notes regarding the role of diet in treating the most common canine health conditions. I've looked through my case histories, talked to colleagues, asked vets whose opinion I respect, and referred to other sources. Almost all of what I am saying can be supported with scientific evidence. But some of it is based on observation, experience and occasionally hearsay.

One should not underestimate the power of food. The wrong food can cause illness and the right food can help cure it. There is a fascinating book on this topic called *How Not to Die* by Michael Greger, which examines the top 15 causes of human death in the USA and explains, with the support of peer-reviewed research, the vital role food plays in human health and longevity. The principles that apply to humans, apply also to dogs. As Hippocrates said: 'Let food be thy medicine and medicine be thy food.'

Mostly Raw

With one or two exceptions (primarily where the dog's immune system has been compromised), you will see that a raw food diet is always recommended. This is because raw food is the easiest thing for your dog to digest and supports his or her immune system. Where raw feeding isn't recommended, you should not revert to processed food but simply cook the ingredients in the way prescribed. Tom Farrington, Chief Veterinary Surgeon for Honey's, believes that processed dog food (including expensive, so-called scientifically developed, brands) is an underlying cause for as many as nine out of ten visits to the vet.

A Reminder About Water

Water plays a crucial role in health. Unfortunately, tap water is treated with a great number of chemicals. Ill dogs are less tolerant of these chemicals, and so it is advisable to find a source of pure, clean water. This could be a mineral water (better from a glass bottle than plastic as plastic bottles left in the sun alter the chemical composition of their contents), rainwater or filtered water.

Why Ill Dogs Do Better On Organic Food

Intensively reared meat and intensively farmed vegetables, especially those imported from developing nations, are likely to contain a surprisingly high percentage of unnatural chemicals (everything from growth hormones to nitrates and from steroids to pesticides). Furthermore, meat will include the residue of whatever the animal has been fed. This is particularly relevant in the case of grain-fed livestock and poultry, and grain is especially harmful to dogs. It is better, therefore, to feed organic food to ill dogs.

A Word About The Gut

A very, very quick biology lesson. Your dog's gastrointestinal (GI) tract has three main functions: digestion, absorption and the prevention of toxins from entering the body. You might think that it is sterile – but it isn't. The intestinal wall is lined with villi (basically, small, finger-like projections) and these, in turn, are covered with bacteria or 'micro-flora'. Good bacteria in the gut are what protects your dog by – amongst other things – producing antibiotics, antivirals and anti-fungals. They also help to control parasites as well as synthesising vital nutrients, co-factors and other essentials for a healthy life.

Your dog's gut is of vital importance to his or her health. The wrong food, medicine and supplements can cause damage to the micro-flora, which in turn can cause

Once your dog has reached his or her target weight you can start a maintenance diet. The quality of the ingredients makes a huge difference.

extremely serious health issues. An obvious example is the damage done by, say, a broad-spectrum antibiotic, which will kill bad and good bacteria alike. On the other hand, the right food will really boost your dog's good bacteria and make a huge difference to his or her health.

If you would like to know more about this whole subject a good place to start is with Professor Tim Spector's book, *The Diet Myth: The Real Science Behind What We Eat*. True, it is all about the human gut, but his key points all apply to dogs. Your dog's gut is one of the key things to consider when planning any medical treatment. The right food – a species-appropriate or raw-food diet – could make a massive difference as could pre- and probiotics (see the separate section to follow).

A Word About The Mouth

In Chapter 7 I mentioned the work done by Drs Gary Beard and Richard Hamlin into the connection in dogs between a healthy mouth and general health or, to be more accurate, the fact that there is a direct correlation between an unhealthy mouth and all sorts of health issues, some of them extremely serious. I mention it again because if your dog has a health issue please give some consideration to his or her mouth. Is there gum disease or infection? Does he or she have cavities or some other oral health issue? It could have a huge outcome on all sorts of apparently unconnected illnesses and diseases.

Free Dietary Advice

I am not a veterinary professional, but my raw dog food company, Honey's, employs vets, vet nurses, nutritionists and other health professionals. We offer a free advisory service to anyone who approaches us – you don't have to be a customer. If you need to see a vet face-to-face we may also be able to make a recommendation.

Prebiotics and probiotics

Dogs, like human beings, have bacteria living in their gut. The bacteria themselves are made up of bad (unfriendly) strains that can make the dog ill and good (friendly) strains that keep it well. Normally, the balance is in favour of the good bacteria, but sometimes – such as after a course of antibiotics, during stress or through poor diet – the bad bacteria get the upper hand. This is called intestinal dysbiosis (see below), a bacterial imbalance that results in an overgrowth of bad bacteria and yeast. Dysbiosis has been linked to various disorders, including yeast infections, irritable bowel disease and rheumatoid arthritis. It is treated by restoring the balance with prebiotics, probiotics and a healthy (natural) diet. Probiotics are beneficial bacteria that can be found in various foods. When you eat probiotics, you will add these healthy bacteria to your intestinal tract. Common strains include the Lactobacillus and Bifidobacterium families of bacteria.Prebiotics, on the other hand, are non-digestible foods that make their way through our digestive system and help good bacteria grow and flourish. Prebiotics keep beneficial bacteria healthy.

Happily, you don't need to buy special canine prebiotics or probiotics, as those designed for humans work perfectly. If you need a prebiotic, try aloe vera or chicory. If you need a probiotic, try one containing Lactobacillus, Acidophilus and/ or Bifidus-type bacteria with FOS (fructooligosaccharides). Use the minimum recommended human dose. Green tripe can be used as a probiotic, as can fermented vegetable.

Conditions Relating To The Digestive System

Acid reflux

Whether raw food is suitable (or whether it would be better to parboil or otherwise cook the ingredients) will depend on whether your dog is on antacid or acid reduction treatment. This is because in order to digest a raw food diet – especially the bone – the stomach's pH needs to be sufficiently high. If your dog has had surgery and isn't taking medication, then raw food with no or minimal bone should be fine. Incidentally, the stomach's pH level can have an effect on the absorption of calcium and vitamin B12, which should be checked regularly when a dog is on antacid or acid reduction treatment.

Bloat and gastric torsion

Since the 1980s, the incidence of bloat, which can lead to gastric torsion, gastric dilatation-volvulus, or GDV, has increased dramatically. In this condition the stomach twists or flips over on itself and gas is trapped. Then any food in the stomach begins to ferment, creating further gases. Later on, circulation to the stomach and spleen are cut off to the point where the dog may go into shock and die. It seems to affect mature, deep-chested dogs the most, especially larger breeds. The condition is extremely serious and potentially fatal.

If you suspect bloat (most common symptoms being an

enlarged abdomen, laboured breathing, excessive drooling, vomiting, a weak pulse, and paleness in the nose and mouth), contact your vet immediately.

For a dog that has suffered and survived bloat, a dry food or kibble diet is definitely not to be recommended. Instead, switch the dog to a raw food diet containing no grains or other fermentable carbohydrates, which is regarded by many vets as preventative. After bloat, many dogs lose weight and it is important to get this back on as soon as possible, since a healthy weight is another factor that reduces risk. Having said this, too much fat in the diet can be harmful. Instead, use lean meat and feed slightly more food, say, three times a day instead of once.

Other tips. Don't exercise your dog right after a meal, and withhold large amounts of water for an hour after eating. Give your pet's body time to process the food he or she has consumed and then offer water in small amounts. If your dog eats very quickly then seek advice on how to slow him or her down. A slower, more even rate of food consumption will help reduce the amount of air your dog swallows, thereby reducing the opportunity for bloat. One of the best things to give dogs that have suffered bloat is (if you can cope with the hygiene and smell issues) green tripe. Avoid vegetables as the fermentation process can produce gas.

It is still not entirely clear why so many dogs appear to be getting bloat. One theory is that dry food is the cause, another theory is that it is stress related. It should always be treated as an emergency. Interestingly, dogs that appear to be happy may be much less prone to this condition.

Colitis

Colitis is either acute or chronic inflammation of the colon and the symptoms aren't terribly pleasant. In acute cases expect vomiting, with diarrhoea containing mucous and blood. In chronic cases the dog will frequently try to pass watery, blood-streaked, mucous and putrid stools. The dog may suffer from flatulence and vomiting. There may be weight loss over time. Do not, however, panic when your vet diagnoses colitis, as it is relatively common and very treatable.

What causes it? Generally speaking, it is the result of eating something unsuitable (perhaps picked up while on a walk), food intolerances or allergies. Other causes can include infection or parasites. Some cases may be stress related, and there is a possibility of an autoimmune cause.

In terms of treatment there is every reason to continue raw feeding since this is the easiest food for your dog to digest. If there is the possibility of a compromised immune system, lightly cook the meat before serving. Avoid high-fat meals, gluten (grains) and dairy products. Use both a prebiotic and a probiotic. A period of fasting may be appropriate.

Constipation

Constipation can occur for many reasons, but especially if a dog becomes dehydrated or has too much bone in his or her diet without sufficient fibre, magnesium or vitamin C.

One of the benefits of a natural diet is that your dog is less likely to become constipated, but if it does become a problem then add more soluble fibre (ripe apple, pears, rose hip or tinned sardines or pilchards), while cutting back on the bone element.

Reduce the number of chicken wings given, if relevant. Incorporating liver or offal into the diet once or twice a week can help. See Chapter 5 for more information.

Coprophagia (eating faeces)

Human beings may find coprophagia (the medical term for eating excrement) disgusting, but to a dog it is a perfectly normal part of their diet. It is believed to have various causes, including:

- The artificial flavouring and appetite stimulants in processed food frequently pass straight through the digestive system without being absorbed into the body. As a result, this can give dog (and cat) faeces a very attractive flavour. It is worth noting that dogs fed pineapple sometimes produce less appealing excrement
- Boredom! This is especially true in the case of younger dogs and those in kennels who may not have enough to occupy them. Regular exercise, companionship and a selection of toys may help
- A mineral or trace element may be lacking from the diet. Adding offal (liver or kidney) to the dog's

diet may provide the missing nutrients. A broad-spectrum supplement for trace minerals such as Dorwest Keeper's Mix may also be of value
• The intestinal flora may be out of balance, possibly as a result of a course of antibiotics. This is especially true if dogs are eating bovine and equine faeces (cow and horse poo, in plain English). A course of prebiotics and probiotics is recommended – perhaps green tripe (if you can face it) or fermented vegetables

Coprophagia can also lead to worms. Worms can also lead to coprophagia. Therefore, treatment against worms may be advisable.

Diarrhoea

There is a huge difference between soft or runny stools and diarrhoea. There is rarely any need to be concerned about soft or runny stools. Diarrhoea, when switching to a raw diet, is also not uncommon for the first few days. True diarrhoea is virtually liquid (like soup) and movements are frequent. There are lots of different reasons for diarrhoea, including:

• Bacterial infection such as salmonella, e. Coli, clostridia and campylobacter
• Viral infection such as parvovirus, distemper and coronavirus
• Yeast infection such as *candida albicans*

- Parasites such as worms, coccidia and protozoa
- Poison
- Tumours
- Stress
- Malabsorption syndromes
- Fungal infection
- Organ failure or inflammation of the pancreas, liver or kidneys

It is obviously important to establish the cause before treatment can be recommended, and to this end it may be necessary to run blood, urine and/or faeces tests. Depending on the seriousness of the condition, the options are to (a) do nothing, (b) fast the dog for a period (c) ask your vet for advice. If it continues for more than 24 hours or if the dog is clearly in pain, young, old or has health issues you should consult a vet immediately.

Here are some tips for dealing with runny stools and diarrhoea:

- Feed a natural, raw diet and plenty of pure, clean water
- Give some prebiotics (see below) to feed the good bacteria in the gut
- Use a probiotic (but ideally not live yoghurt). See below for details
- Try to avoid antibiotics, steroids and anti-inflammatory drugs unless the dog is seriously ill
- If it is a long-term issue and your dog is otherwise healthy you could try slippery elm or a modest

amount of brewer's yeast to aid digestion. Psyllium husk is another option

- Try a remedy such as Ferrum Phosphoricum 12× or 6× tissue salt to help slow the diarrhoea and increase absorption
- Add bone broth to food as it provides electrolytes and rehydrates as well as being easy to digest

Please note that gluten, cereals, cereal by-products and modified starch all contribute to canine digestive problems. Make sure your dog has plenty of water to avoid dehydration.

Dysbiosis aka Leaky gut

Dysbiosis, which is also referred to as 'leaky gut', although confusingly the definitions are slightly different, basically refers to a bacterial imbalance that leads to inflammation of the intestinal mucosa (the lining of the GI tract). Once inflamed, the intestinal lining is compromised and allows undigested food particles and other potential toxins to enter the bloodstream. The overuse of antibiotics, steroids and other drugs is one of the biggest causes but there are others including processed food, vaccines, stress and parasite infections. Typical symptoms include flatulence, bloating and diarrhoea. It can also cause or exacerbate a wide range of other – seemingly unconnected – conditions from gum disease to joint pain and from seizures to asthma. It is my feeling that it is often the cause of allergic dermatitis, inflamed ears, red skin, itchiness, scabs, hotspots, and general redness. It is one of the main reasons why I opened this chapter with a section on the importance of keeping your dog's gut healthy.

Treatment is not always easy. Dogs with dysbiosis have fragile immune and digestive systems. The first step is to consider any food allergies or intolerances and to look at any underlying nutritional deficiencies caused by mal absorption or inefficient digestion. Appropriate probiotics, enzymes and nutraceuticals may be required. Probiotics are especially important as they will reintroduce good bacteria and prevent an overgrowth of bad bacteria.

However, you must choose carefully, as some dogs can't tolerate dairy-based, yeast-based or even non-dairy probiotics. The importance of stopping highly processed dog food cannot be over-emphasised. Instead, opt for a balanced, species-appropriate diet. Remember, your dog may be intolerant to certain protein sources and a certain amount of experimentation may be required.

Flatulence

All dogs, regardless of their diet, are likely to have a certain amount of flatulence. The most frequent cause is the carbohydrates in processed food – easily remedied by a switch to natural feeding. Antibiotics may also be responsible, in which case a course of probiotics will often help. A small percentage of dogs produce wind as a result of eating vegetables, or particular vegetables, and this can be dealt with by reducing the percentage of vegetables being served or excluding them completely.

Inflammatory bowel disease

Inflammatory bowel disease (IBD) is similar to Crohn's disease in humans and is diagnosed in dogs with greater frequency. It is a chronic inflammatory intestinal disease that can occur anywhere in the digestive tract, but most commonly involves the small intestine and colon.

What should you watch out for? Recurrent bouts of diarrhoea, that is sometimes watery, explosive, odd-coloured (yellowish), mucous-coated, slimy and often has blood streaks. Vomiting (sometimes blood-tinged) is not unusual and the dog may have abdominal pain with distension to the bowel and abdomen. The stomach may emit gurgling noises. Dogs are often lethargic with weight loss and may have an increase or loss of appetite. As these symptoms are similar to other conditions it can be difficult to make a positive diagnosis without a gut biopsy.

In terms of treatment there is every reason to start or continue raw feeding, since this is the easiest food for your dog to digest. However, reduce the fat content, avoid all grains and dairy products and increase the amount of fibre, such as psyllium husk. Slippery elm can help, too. Use both a prebiotic and a probiotic. Probiotics in the form of fermented foods such as green tripe, Kefir, sauerkraut and yoghurt will help balance the gut flora especially after a long course of antibiotics.

Please note: If your dog is taking a course of Salazopyrin we would not recommend raw feeding but instead suggest cooking the same ingredients. Also, if he or she has any digestive tract ulcers we would suggest waiting for these to heal before switching to a raw food diet (again, you could cook the ingredients). Bone broth can help to reduce inflammation in the bowel.

Irritable bowel syndrome

Irritable bowel syndrome (IBS) is difficult to diagnose because so many of the symptoms, which may be intermittent, are shared with other conditions. You should watch out for intermittent bouts of diarrhoea or soft stools, increased frequency of defecation, small stools, straining to defecate, abdominal distension (bloating), flatulence, weight loss and, sometimes, regurgitation of food. The stomach may emit gurgling noises. It is believed that diet and stress are the main causes, with some drugs aggravating an already sensitive digestive system.

In terms of treatment there is every reason to start or continue raw feeding since this is the easiest food for your dog to digest. If there is the possibility of a compromised immune system then lightly cook the food before serving. Follow the same advice as for IBD.

Vomiting

It is important to remember that dogs regularly regurgitate their food, and this process should not be confused with vomiting that is due to a potential or underlying health issue.

If a dog vomits repeatedly and/or seems unwell in other ways then it warrants contacting a vet. However, if the dog isn't vomiting repeatedly and has no other apparent symptoms, you may like to start by fasting him or her for 24 hours, ensuring that there is an ample supply of pure, clean water available throughout. If your dog seems to be over-drinking or having trouble keeping water down then give him or her a block of ice, which will thaw slowly, ensuring a constant but reduced supply of water.

Assuming the dog has stopped vomiting after 24 hours, offer a small, light meal. This can consist of scrambled egg or cooked chicken with a prebiotic and a probiotic. You could also try a little bone broth. If vomiting doesn't reoccur then towards the end of the second day serve a smaller-than-usual meal of whatever the dog normally eats. Resume your ordinary schedule of feeding on day three.

Please note: If vomiting continues or is constant, or if it contains blood or if it is in tandem with diarrhoea, consult your vet immediately.

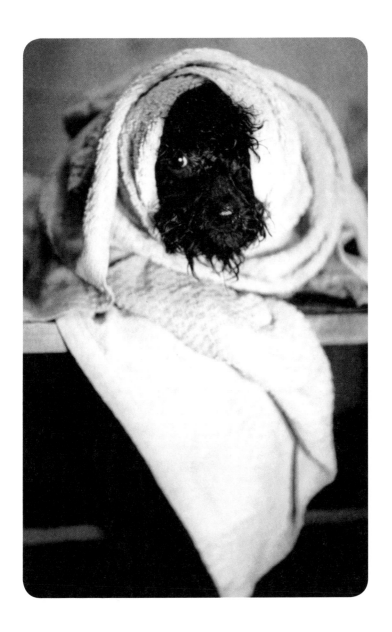

The thyroid gland made easy

Why do vets (and doctors for that matter) go on about the connection between the thyroid gland and weight? The thyroid gland is responsible for something called the 'metabolic rate'. In very, very plain English this is the rate at which your body burns energy. It achieves this with the aid of a series of hormones called, with staggering originality, the thyroid hormones (how do they come up with these names?). These are, in turn, stimulated by a thyroid-stimulating hormone from the pituitary gland and require trace amounts of iodine.

Enough science. The real point is that poor thyroid function can produce all sorts of symptoms including weight gain, lassitude, depression and other behavioural changes. Other symptoms could include dry skin, hair loss, thickening or discoloration of the skin, bacterial skin infections, chronic infections (including ear infections), neck pain and seizures.

What causes the thyroid to act up? It can be a side-effect of medication (especially of steroids), exposure to toxins (including vaccines), neutering and lack of exercise. Most dogs that develop hypothyroidism (the medical term for all of this) do so between the ages of 4 and 10. If your dog develops hypothyroidism it is worth asking your vet to look also for underlying adrenal gland stress.

What else should you know? There are a number of ways to measure the thyroid health of your pup through blood tests with 'T' names like free T3, free T4, T3, T4, AAT3, AAT4 and TSH. Should your dog be diagnosed with autoimmune thyroiditis he or she will probably need to have medication to replace the thyroid hormone for the rest of their life, but there is still much you can do.

Most vets in the UK only test for T4 and TSH in routine blood tests and can therefore miss these cases. For this reason, I generally recommend a more in-depth blood test. Someone who knows a great deal about this is Jean Dodd at HemoPet (*www.hemopet.org*) and if your own vet has trouble making a clear diagnosis I would consider asking for a referral.

Usually by the time your pet has enough auto-antibodies to be measured on a blood test there has been irreparable thyroid damage and synthetic hormone replacement is almost always inevitable. However, if there's no autoimmune disorder present, it may be possible to stimulate the remaining thyroid tissue to begin working again. If your dog's thyroid glands have taken early retirement, which is confirmed by low thyroid levels on blood work, it may be possible the thyroid can be regenerated using a more natural form of thyroid replacement such as adding pork or beef thyroid gland to food. Other ideas our vet has suggested include avoiding any ingredient containing gluten or other hormone disrupters.

Internal Conditions

Addison's disease

Addison's disease is the opposite of Cushing's syndrome in as much that the adrenal gland does not produce enough corticosteroid. It can be a side-effect of the drugs used to treat Cushing's. It is less common than Cushing's and can lead to other health issues.

The adrenal gland secretes several substances that help regulate normal bodily functions. Some of the most important products are glucocorticoids and mineralocorticoids. Glucocorticoids such as cortisol have an effect on sugar, fat and protein metabolism. Mineralocorticoids such as aldosterone help to regulate blood pressure and allow the kidneys to maintain a proper water–salt balance in the body (by helping the kidneys retain sodium and excrete potassium). If the adrenal glands are not functioning properly, and the production level of aldosterone drops, a drop in blood pressure and severe dehydration can occur. Dysfunctioning adrenal glands are the main cause of Addison's disease.

Symptoms include muscle weakness and general lethargy, diarrhoea and vomiting, hyperpigmentation, joint pain, lack of appetite and muscle shivers and tremors. The usual treatment is hormone replacement with drugs such as fludrocortisone.

Diet should be under veterinary supervision. Changes in the health of the patient may require a change of diet and this will only be known if blood is monitored. Avoid vegetables and other foods high in vitamin A (such as carrots, celery and liver), also foods high in potassium (bananas, most meats but especially pork). Raw chicken or turkey are excellent as they have lower potassium levels. Salt (high sodium rather than sea salt or low sodium) will generally have to be added to the diet, but this will depend on the blood analysis. Fresh adrenal gland in the diet can be beneficial as can dehydrated adrenal gland as a supplement. It is important that the patient is not stressed. Some herbal and homeopathic remedies can help to achieve this. Patients may also benefit from a small amount of quinoa or porridge – as well as chia seeds, cottage cheese, tuna, egg, sunflower or pumpkin seeds, raw walnuts and raw almonds. The most important thing is to stabilise and maintain sodium levels.

Cushing's syndrome

Cushing's syndrome is an enlargement of the adrenal glands resulting in increased production of adrenocortical hormones. Symptoms are increased thirst, appetite and the need to urinate. With time the dog can develop a potbelly and an intolerance to exercise with some cases showing muscle spasms and difficulty bending their legs. The coat becomes dry, hairs fine and the skin thins. Hair loss around the flanks and abdomen can spread to the legs, back and head. The diet has to be easy on the liver and help the thyroid gland. High-fat diets should be avoided and the best recipes to follow are chicken with some offal, rabbit and chicken mixed together, venison or lean beef. In terms of vegetables carrot is excellent (for the beta carotene) as are broccoli, garlic and grapefruit seed extract. The best supplement to help the thyroid is kelp or a similar seaweed. For the liver add milk thistle and for the heart (patients are likely to suffer from raised cholesterol) add hawthorn. The addition of fresh adrenal gland and/or dehydrated gland powder can also help stabilise these cases.

The diet and supplements need to be changed radically should the patient slip from Cushing's to Addison's. Other supplements that will help patients with Cushing's include vitamins A and D (cod liver oil), vitamin B6, folic acid, vitamin C, vitamin K, calcium, magnesium, potassium, selenium, brewer's yeast and zinc. However, you should not add extra supplements to the diet without consulting a vet. Herbal and homeopathic vets have much to offer in the treatment.

Diabetes mellitus

Diabetes mellitus (aka Type II) occurs when the pancreas doesn't produce enough insulin or because cells do not respond to the insulin that is produced. Insulin is required for the body to efficiently use sugars, fats and proteins. The commonest symptoms are increased thirst and urination. One of the leading causes of Type II diabetes is being overweight. Another lifestyle reason why dogs can develop diabetes is lack of exercise. In many cases cataracts (cloudy lenses in the eyes) may be the first sign that there is a problem. This disease may occur in conjunction with Cushing's syndrome, urinary tract infections, hypothyroidism, pancreatitis and cancer. The condition is usually diagnosed from a urine or blood test.

According to Dr Karen Becker there is a growing body of research that connects autoimmune disorders to Type II diabetes, especially in dogs. If your dog's immune system attacks the pancreas, he or she can develop diabetes. One of the reasons why this may happen is the annual round of vaccinations that your vet may be encouraging you to have. These are often unnecessary – especially if your dog had a complete set of shots as a puppy. Instead, I would recommend having something called titer testing done.

- A titer test is a laboratory test measuring the existence and level of antibodies to disease in blood. Antibodies are produced when an antigen (like a virus or bacteria) provokes a response from the immune system. This response can come from natural exposure or from vaccination

- Source: Jan Rasmusen, *Dog Vaccinations* (courtesy of *Dog's Naturally* magazine)

Titer results will tell you whether re-vaccination is necessary, and for exactly which disease.

If there is one condition where switching to a natural, raw food diet can prove really effective it is diabetes. However, the switch needs to be made carefully if you are taking your dog off a modern high-carbohydrate commercial diet and I would definitely recommend doing it under veterinary supervision.

If antibiotics are used as part of conventional treatment then prebiotics and probiotics are recommended. A holistic vet may also suggest other treatments including extra vitamins (Vitamin E has proven effective in treating Type II diabetes in humans), Chinese herbs, supplements and acupuncture. The most important thing – and I can't stress this sufficiently – is diet and exercise.

Exocrine pancreatic insufficiency

Exocrine pancreatic insufficiency (EPI) is the inability to properly digest food due to a lack of digestive enzymes made by the pancreas. It affects German Shepherds more than any other breed (about two-thirds of cases). EPI is caused by a progressive loss of the pancreatic cells that make digestive enzymes. It is often not diagnosed until well advanced. Symptoms include weight loss, poor hair coat, flatulence and a voracious appetite. Sufferers may also pass bulky, fatty stools.

In terms of treatment there is every reason to start or continue raw feeding since this is the easiest food for your dog to digest. The amount of fat consumed should be kept to a minimum: chicken and lean beef are both good. Avoid any food (including cooked vegetables such as carrots and peas) containing a high proportion of sugar as this forces the pancreas to work harder. Digestive enzymes and Tree Barks Powder can help. Keep the amount of fibre to a minimum (it affects how effective the added enzymes are). Holistic vets may recommend that you add fresh, raw pancreas (sheep, cow, pig or game) and this can make a huge difference. By the way, it is fine to freeze the fresh, raw pancreas and thaw it as necessary. Coconut oil is recommended in some individuals with hereditary EPI; this provides extra calories in the form of medium chain triglycerides. It is important to make sure your dog has plenty of pure, clean water. In the long term, after the gut wall recovers, dogs with hereditary EPI can be maintained on a normal fat level in most cases.

Liver disease including Hepatitis

The liver has five important functions, affecting circulation, excretion of waste products, metabolism, immunological defence and blood formation. There are two types of liver disease: primary and secondary. Primary is caused by a non- or sub-functioning liver; secondary is caused by some other condition, such as bacteria, viral parasites, poisons, toxins or tumours.

The most common symptoms associated with liver disease include loss of appetite, vomiting, abdominal pain, enlarged liver, jaundice, discoloured urine, oedema (swelling), weight loss, photosensitisation (skin disease related to sunlight), poor blood clotting, anaemia and a change in stools (either diarrhoea or constipation). Once the cause has been treated, diet has an important role to play, especially in relation to the carbohydrate, fat, protein, vitamin and mineral content. Raw feeding is ideal. Avoid all dairy and stick to a low-fat diet. Conventional treatment can lead to a compromised immune system, in which case food should be lightly cooked. If antibiotics have been used as part of the treatment then it is advisable to give your dog prebiotics and probiotics.

Impacted anal glands

Impacted anal glands are an extremely common problem for dogs. The glands are situated either side of the anus and discharge a foul-smelling liquid, which is used for marking territories. They are usually emptied by the passing of firm stools, or if the animal becomes frightened. If not emptied frequently they become impacted, which leads to infection and possibly an abscess being formed. Many vets feel that the primary cause of this problem is processed dog food.

If your dog licks under their tail a great deal, especially if it causes eczema, or if they drag their bottom along the ground, this could well be an anal gland problem. (However, the same symptoms could also be caused by worms or even fleas.)

One of the benefits of a natural diet incorporating bone is that it creates small, firm stools, which empty the anal glands as the dog excretes.

Kidney disease (renal failure)

There are two types of canine kidney failure – acute and chronic. Acute renal failure comes on suddenly in response to a precipitating event such as swallowing a poisonous plant or drinking anti-freeze. Chronic renal failure is a slower process and may take months or years to develop. It is most commonly seen in older dogs. Unfortunately, chronic renal insufficiency usually happens so gradually that by the time the symptoms become obvious, it's often too late to treat the problem effectively. Symptoms to watch for include:

- Increased thirst
- Increased urination
- Decreased or lack of urination
- Urinating during the night
- Bloody urine
- Vomiting and/or diarrhoea
- Hunched posture; reluctance to move
- Poor coat condition
- Weight loss
- Mouth ulcers and bad breath
- Dehydration
- High blood pressure
- Anaemia
- Fluid retention in limbs and abdomen
- Small, large or painful kidneys

Perhaps the first and most important point to make is that dogs suffering from this disease are more likely to become dehydrated due to the reduced ability of the kidneys to conserve water. Maintaining a good fluid intake may help slow the progression of kidney disease. Encourage your dog to drink lots of water – consider adding it to the food and even flavouring it by adding, for example, a little goats' milk. Using filtered water or rainwater may encourage drinking.

Renal failure is one of those conditions where the switch to a raw food diet definitely needs to be done with professional support.

Generally speaking, a raw food diet is excellent with the added benefit that it contains such a high percentage of water. However, there are instances where your vet may recommend parboiling ingredients, possibly with lots of water and extra vegetables (especially green vegetables). The extra vegetables will, incidentally, reduce the level of animal protein. When cooking the meat, heat it until it changes colour and then leave it to finish cooking using its own heat.

Patients with chronic kidney disease should have a low quantity of high-quality protein. By 'low quantity' I mean the amount required for that dog and no extra. Raw meat contains relatively more and higher-quality protein than prescription kidney diets and most kibbles. However, unlike cereal-based highly processed foods, the protein in raw meat is easily broken down into amino acids that are useful. Therefore, don't be fooled by what it says on many low-protein, processed dog foods.

As phosphate is another component that relies solely on extraction by the kidneys, a lower phosphate diet is also recommended for these pets. Raw meat cannot compete with prescription diets on phosphate content; nevertheless a vet can prescribe phosphate binders which stop phosphate absorption in the intestines and therefore reduce the workload on the kidney. There may also be some benefit to adding water-soluble vitamins to the diet as these are often lost in excess urine loss. Adding colourful fruits and vegetables, juiced or mashed, will help replace these losses.

A supplement called Udo's Beyond Greens can help throughput and to balance out the urea. Add it once the food has cooled and is ready to serve so as not to destroy the nutrients. Where high blood pressure is an issue, test to see whether calcium, magnesium, potassium and sodium are all in the middle of the normal range. If below this level, consider adding supplements. Cod liver oil, zinc and magnesium are very important dietary additions for patients with high blood pressure. *Solidago* (also called goldenrods) can also be of assistance. See below for more about urinary stones and purine problems.

Liver shunt

The medical term for liver shunt is portosystemic shunt (PSS). A 'shunt' is a blood vessel that bypasses the liver rather than passing through it. Dogs can be born with the condition or it may be acquired. Small dogs are affected more than larger dogs. Diet has an important role to play in the treatment of liver shunt. Normally, the liver removes ammonia from the bloodstream so when this isn't happening it is important to stop the body from producing ammonia in the first place. This can partly be achieved by a low-protein diet. Adding drugs like lactulose and ursodiol to the diet helps with this problem. Make sure the dog drinks plenty of water in order to avoid dehydration.

Avoid fasting your dog as this will result in more

ammonia in the system as the body breaks down its own protein. Feeding little and often (perhaps four to six times daily) will help with this. Avoid high-fat recipes; medium and low will be suitable. Add extra fruits for carbohydrate (sugars) as it will prevent the liver from having to work at making its own (gluconeogenesis).

Homeopathic support for the liver can be very helpful and should be done under veterinary supervision. Low-potency organ support remedies such as chelidonium, *Carduus marianus*, *Taraxacum* and *Berberis* are recommended. In some cases, adding carbohydrate to the diet in the form of organic porridge oats soaked overnight in water can assist in reducing the protein percentage in the diet. Other suitable carbohydrate additions are polenta and brown rice.

Pancreatitis

The pancreas is a V-shaped organ located behind the stomach and the first section of the small intestine, known as the duodenum. It performs two main functions: it aids in the metabolism of sugar in the body through the production of insulin and is necessary for the digestion of food by producing pancreatic enzymes. Inflammation of the pancreas is called pancreatitis. The symptoms of the disease are a painful abdomen, abdominal distension, poor appetite, depression, dehydration, vomiting, diarrhoea and yellow, greasy stools. The dog may also look 'hunched up'.

There are various causes of pancreatitis, including certain medications, infections, metabolic disorders (high amounts of lipid or calcium in the blood), trauma and shock. Middle-aged dogs and dogs with diets high in fat and/or carbohydrates seem to be at most risk. It is thought that dogs who suffer from Cushing's disease (hyperadrenocorticism), hyperthyroidism and diabetes may also be at risk.

In terms of treatment there is every reason to start or continue raw feeding since this is the easiest food for your dog to digest. The amount of fat consumed should be kept to a minimum: chicken and lean beef are both good. Avoid any food (including vegetables such as cooked parsnips and cooked carrots) containing a high proportion of sugar, as this forces the pancreas to work harder. Small amounts of bone broth with any excess fat removed can be used to rehydrate, where necessary.

If the pancreas is totally non-functional or very sub-functional, medical supplements such as enzyme replacements may be necessary. This can be done with conventional enzyme replacements or herbal supplements (such as Tree Barks Powder from Dorwest Herbs). Some holistic vets will also suggest fresh raw pancreas.

Patients may also need antibiotics or steroids as part of a conventional treatment. One problem with conventional treatment is that patients can become immunocompromised as a result of the steroids, meaning that they will be more susceptible to infection even from the relatively normal bacteria in raw food. In such a case the food should be lightly cooked first.

Weight control is particularly important. Keep your dog trim.

Bladder and kidney stones and the purine problem

Bladder and kidney stones are formed when mineral crystals in the urine clump together and form small stones which gradually increase in size. They cause inflammation in the kidney or bladder and if large enough can cause a blockage of the bladder or get lodged in the urinary tract. Some breeds are more prone to the formation of bladder stones. Stones form more easily when dogs do not drink plenty of water, and so are more commonly seen in dogs fed on dry food diets. Stones also form more easily if there are bacteria in the urine. Some stones form more easily in slightly acid urine (such as oxalate), others form readily in alkaline urine (such as struvite). Struvite and oxalate are the two commonest types of bladder stones; others less often found are cystine and urate. Stones can sometimes be dissolved by a change in diet but large stones may need surgery to remove them.

If you have a Dalmatian, Beagle, Bulldog, Basset Hound, Cocker Spaniel, Bichon Frise, Miniature Schnauzer, Lhasa Apso, Miniature Poodle, Yorkshire Terrier, Miniature Schnauzer, Dachshund, Newfoundland, Irish Terrier, Scottish Terrier or Irish Setter then you are probably only too aware that these breeds can have purine metabolism problems.

What are purines?

Purines are natural substances found in plant and animal cells that are vital to the chemical structure of genes. High levels of purine can be found in any food group (i.e. vegetables, fruit, meat and fish). Certain foods, such as kidneys, game, yeast, mackerel, herring, sardines and mussels have particularly high levels of purine. Others, such as chicken, beef, lamb and non-acidic fruit, contain lower levels.

When cells die and get recycled in a dog's body the purines in their genetic material also get broken down. Once completely broken down they turn into uric acid, which is important to good health because it serves as an antioxidant that protects blood vessels.

However, sometimes uric acid levels in the blood and other parts of the body can become too high. This happens, for instance, when the kidney isn't functioning properly (as it is the kidney that helps keep blood levels of uric acid balanced) or where there is an excessive breakdown of cells. Although kidneys regulate the amount of purine (excreting what isn't required), it is worth remembering that the cause of the problem lies in the liver where purine metabolism takes place.

Purine problems in dogs

The breeds already mentioned above metabolise purine in a unique way ending up with excess uric acid. This in turn leads to urate stones, which may lodge in the bladder or kidney. Worse, if treated with allopurinol to block enzyme-producing urates, dogs can end up with xanthine stones instead of urate stones.

Urate stones are radiolucent and thus can easily be missed, especially when in the kidneys as X-rays pass right through them, leaving no shadow, unlike other stones. It takes air contrast X-rays to show them up. But this cannot be done in the kidney and the stone cannot be felt in the kidney, either. Even ultrasound can miss them but CT (computerised tomography) scanning can pick them up.

If you have a Dalmatian
Dalmatians are one breed that has been particularly prone to urinary stones and if you have a Dalmatian or are interested in why, then this site will be of interest: www.thedca.org/ stonecharts.html.

How can diet help?
It is important to note that different diet recommendations will vary depending on the type of stone.

A raw food diet without organ meat and with none of the high-purine vegetables (such as cauliflower, peas, spinach, mushrooms and legumes) is generally excellent as a diet for all breeds with a purine metabolism problem. Some commercial and homemade low-purine diets can make the condition worse rather than better. If your dog has cystine stones the amino acid content in a raw diet can make it unsuitable and so cooking the same, high-quality ingredients is generally recommended.

In compromised dogs a high-fat diet can add to the problems by increasing urate formation, especially in the kidneys. So if you have a thin dog with a purine problem, consider increasing the frequency and size of meals rather than the fat level, and check for hidden stones.

Bear in mind that plenty of pure water is also important. The word 'pure' must be emphasised, as some additions to water for purification and sterilisation purposes can change the urine pH or entire body chemistry, triggering crystal formation.

What else? 'Table foods' are out and so is anything with salt in it. With regard to diet, incidentally, this may require the addition of potassium citrates (for preventing calcium oxalate crystals). Always ensure that the diet does not have excessive amounts of vitamin C (ascorbic acid) added, as it acidifies urine, decreasing the risk of the most common forms of stones but increasing the risk of urates.

Finally, do remember to arrange regular urine checks to ensure that the pH stays at the correct level for the type of stones your dog is prone to.

Oral Conditions

Gingivitis

Gingivitis is an infection and/or inflammation of the gums and is often caused by the build-up of plaque on the teeth. Symptoms include bad breath, a sore mouth and consequent loss of appetite. Prevention is better than cure and chewing regularly on bones is to be recommended. There is a close connection between oral health and general health. There is every reason, therefore, to feed a raw diet.

Halitosis (bad breath)

The most common causes of bad breath are poor diet or poor oral health. The latter could be caused by bacteria, saliva and food particles forming plaque. A worse problem is periodontal disease, which can lead to gingivitis. Other possible causes include diabetes, kidney disease, gastro-intestinal disease and infections in the area around the mouth. Respiratory diseases (for instance a sinus infection) and other oral diseases may be responsible. Finally, one should not rule out something that the dog is eating, such as household waste (or worse!). Obviously, the treatment will depend on the cause. Good dental hygiene can be achieved by chewing regularly on bones.

Skin Conditions

Alopecia (fur loss)

There are many reasons why dogs may lose their coats. Some of the more common causes are allergies, bacterial, fungal or viral infections, mites and poor diet. Trauma to the skin from scratching, burns or wounds as well as stress and hormonal changes (as seen in Cushing's syndrome) may also be responsible. Dietary advice will depend on the underlying condition. A raw food diet is almost always beneficial, especially where the underlying cause may be an allergy, bacterial or fungal infection.

Itchy ears and skin problems caused by allergies

Itchiness, ear infections, fur loss and skin problems may be caused by a variety of issues, the most common of which is an allergy to food, grains, fleas, ticks, household chemicals, pollen or something else.

If the problem is a food allergy it could well be the result of eating grain or grain-fed meat (intensively reared beef and chicken are often responsible). Traditionally, vets have treated ear and skin problems of this type with a course of antibiotics and steroids, desensitising injections and various creams.

Before treatment can be started, it is important to identify the cause of the allergy. In the case of any food allergy the switch to a natural diet may solve the problem, especially as it will help to support the immune system. If the patient has taken antibiotics, a course of prebiotics and probiotics is recommended. One of the ways in which the body responds to a skin-related allergy is to release histamine and other chemicals. Omega-3 can, sometimes, reduce the effects of histamine. Note that other fatty acids, such as the majority of omega-6s, can actually worsen some allergies.

Itchy skin

Apart from allergies (see above), there are many different reasons why dogs suffer from itchy skin, including mites, demodex and mange. Until the cause is known, it is difficult to recommend a treatment, but the following tips may help:

- Various oils reduce inflammation, including cod liver oil, evening primrose oil and starflower oil

- Consider adding vitamin C to the diet. At least 1000mg daily and even more if the dog can absorb it without diarrhoea

- If you are taking a dog off medication, use a broad-spectrum multivitamin that includes magnesium as this will dampen down the side-effects

- If the dog has been given antibiotics, a course of prebiotics and probiotics is recommended

Homeopathic remedies can be very helpful alongside conventional medicine in these cases.

Paw chewing

If your dog is chewing its paws, the first step is to check that there are no foreign bodies, such as eggshell splinters, thorns or glass, present and that he or she hasn't sustained a cut. If the dog is on processed food, the cause may be dietary since a grain allergy can produce this symptom. A raw food diet is to be recommended. If the cause is boredom then giving the dog a bone may solve the problem. If persistent, check the dog's urine for a kidney problem. It may also be worth checking for a thyroid problem. Finally, it may be the result of blocked anal sacs or an allergy either to some ingredient in his or her food or even to an environmental factor such as contact with, say, household cleaners or stinging nettles.

Other Conditions

Arthritis

Depending upon who you talk to, the terms 'arthritis', 'osteoarthritis' and 'degenerative joint disease' may or may not be used to describe the same thing. Degenerative joint disease is characterised by the loss of the smooth cartilage that covers and protects the ends of the bones in a movable joint. The cartilage has no nerves so when it touches the cartilage of another bone there is no pain. When the cartilage wears away, the bone is exposed and, since bones do have nerves, pain and inflammation are caused by the two ends in a joint touching each other. This is the sign that arthritis is present and will probably be progressive. In degenerative joint disease, small bony projections known as osteophytes form on the bone that is closest to the joint.

Degenerative joint disease can occur as a result of wear and tear on an otherwise normal joint and occurs as the dog ages. Osteoarthritis may also occur as a result of hip dysplasia or elbow dysplasia.

A raw food diet helps arthritis because it is low in carbohydrates. High-carbohydrate diets create an excessively acid bloodstream, decreasing uric acid solubility, which in turn leads to joint pain. Bones are an important part of the diet and should include joint bones for their cartilage content (high in chondroitin sulphate) and the marrow of bones including chicken (chicken bones have lots of glucosamine, as does beef trachea). Turkey is also a good source and, importantly, much lower in salt than most commercial supplements. Such a diet often does away with the need for such supplements as glucosamine and chondroitin, or lowers the required dose.

Supplements that help arthritic pets include cod liver, evening primrose and starflower oil, vitamin C, green-lipped mussel, turmeric, ginger and boswellia (between $1/16$th and $1/8$th of a teaspoon only), black treacle (also known as blackstrap molasses), and the herbs devil's and cat's claw.

Cancers and tumours

One of the ways in which many cancers and tumours can be starved is to reduce the carbohydrates in the diet to 20% or under. (Bear in mind that many commercial dog foods may contain 60% or more carbohydrates.) The purity of the food – ideally it should be organic – and the water is crucial. The vegetables should be as fresh as possible as after a few days vegetables start to lose their nutritional value. Of the many different supplements that can help cancer patients, vitamin C is perhaps the most important: 1000mg a day (or more) is recommended.

Please contact Honey's Real Dog Food if you would like more specific advice.

Discospondylitis

Discospondylitis (diskospondylitis or vertebral osteomyelitis) is a bacterial or fungal infection of the vertebrae and the intervertebral discs. The resulting inflammation and swelling along with the bone deformities put pressure on the spinal cord, which runs through the vertebrae. Feed the dog a natural diet. Supplements to consider include vitamins B12, E, C and zinc. Give the dog a natural probiotic.

Elbow dysplasia

Elbow dysplasia is more common in fast-growing larger-breed dogs while they are still puppies. Dogs with elbow dysplasia usually have a limp and may hold the leg out from the body when walking. Some will avoid putting any weight on the leg at all. As many sufferers mature, the symptoms may become less severe. Medication may be needed to reduce pain. Some dogs may need surgery and others will have an altered elbow joint with arthritis from a young age. Feed a raw food diet with plenty of bone such as chicken wings, chicken thighs, drumsticks, pork ribs and marrowbones. Supplement with oil (fish, evening primrose or hemp oil) and vitamin C. Do not allow the dog to over-exercise.

Epilepsy

Epilepsy is a disorder of recurring seizures. Epileptic fits are the result of a sort of short-circuiting of the nerves in the brain, so that many nerves are stimulated at once. This can result in quite violent body spasms. Not all dogs that have seizures are epileptic; fits can happen for a number of reasons. For example, older dogs may have an underlying heart, kidney or liver condition, or there may be a tumour on the brain. Traumatic injuries to the head can lead to fits in any age dog, as can infections, such as viral or bacterial ones. Occasionally, poisons such as slug pellets (metaldehyde) will cause a dog to fit. In any of the above cases it is important to treat the underlying problem, if possible, and so eliminate or control the fits that way.

Diet has an important role to play in the treatment of epilepsy. Meats low in glutamate, such as lamb, are best. Avoid meat from animals that have been fed a grain diet. Avoid rabbit, turkey and oily fish, as all are high in glutamate. Epilepsy is definitely on the rise and the combination of wheat and soy in pet foods may well be responsible. Eggs (again low in glutamate) are a good source of nutrition. In addition to the above, one should try to ensure the diet is free of chemicals (preservatives, taste enhancers, palatability factors, chemical antioxidants and so forth), making organic ingredients ideal. Processed foods are particularly bad for epileptic dogs as they are high in grain and incorporate rancid fats. Some vets recommend adding coconut oil to the food.

Hip dysplasia

Hip dysplasia is associated with abnormal joint structure and a laxity in the muscles, connective tissue and ligaments that normally support the joint. As the laxity develops, the head of the femur and socket joint separate. This is known as subluxation. Most dogs are born with normal hips; however, owing to their genetic makeup and possibly other factors, the soft tissues surrounding the joint develop abnormally, causing subluxation that leads to altered gait and/or lameness. One or both hips may be affected. Feed a raw food diet with plenty of bone such as chicken wings, chicken thighs, drumsticks, pork ribs and marrowbones. Supplement with oil (fish, evening primrose or hemp oil) and vitamin C. Do not allow the dog to over-exercise.

Luxating patella

Luxating patella only occurs in certain breeds, particularly small dogs with short legs. When it occurs, the leg locks up with the foot held off the ground. It cannot return to its normal position until the quadriceps muscle relaxes and increases in length. Typically, a small dog will be running and then in mid-stride yelp, hold up the back leg and then continue as if nothing is wrong. After a time, the leg drops back down and is used normally. The lameness is very intermittent and does not seem to worry the dog. A raw food diet is excellent. Ensure plenty of bone. Keep the dog from becoming overweight as this will worsen the symptoms.

Osteochondritis dissecans

Osteochondritis dissecans, or OCD (not obsessive–compulsive disorder!), is a disease of the cartilage which may affect the shoulder, elbow, knee or hock. Some dogs will barely have a limp, while others may not want to put any weight on the affected leg. Lameness can worsen after exercise and improves after resting.

It is caused by many factors, including genetics, trauma, rapid growth and poor nutrition. The conventional treatment is strict rest, an NSAID (non-steroidal anti-inflammatory drug) such as carprofen, or surgery to remove the damaged cartilage.

It is important that the dog does not become overweight. Feed a raw food diet. Ensure plenty of bone. Supplements which may help include oil (fish, evening primrose, starflower and/or hemp) and vitamin C.

Spondylosis

Spondylosis is a non-infectious fusion or degeneration of the vertebrae. The dog is stiff after getting up, appears to be limping (especially after exercise) or begins snapping or licking the lower back. Occasionally, a bony spur or fusing of the vertebrae will cause loss of bladder control and the dog will become incontinent. Feed the dog a natural diet. Supplements to consider include turmeric, ginger, boswellic acids, cat's claw, devil's claw, green-lipped mussel, cod liver oil and glucosamine. Also consider vitamins B12, C, E and zinc. It is important that the dog isn't allowed to jump up or go up and down stairs too frequently.

A word about steroids

Steroids can produce unpleasant side-effects (including lethargy, excessive hunger, excessive thirst and osteoporosis) and may even cause diabetic-type syndrome. Before putting your dog on a course of steroids, consider consulting a holistic vet to see what other options are available.

13

SUPPORT FOR THE LUCKY DOG WEIGHT LOSS PLAN

13

SUPPORT FOR THE LUCKY DOG WEIGHT LOSS PLAN

After I had finished writing *The Lucky Dog Weight Loss Plan* I sent the manuscript to a number of vets whose opinion I especially valued. Their comments (and contact details) are to be found below. You can rest assured that the Lucky Dog Weight Loss Plan is approved and supported by leading members of the veterinary profession. Incidentally, if you are ever looking for a good vet please do contact my office as we keep details of vets with natural feeding experience.

• 'A wonderful, detailed and well written book that we feel confident in recommending to our clients. Tackling a very important subject in a sensitive yet well-informed way. With more than 80% of our clients now feeding raw food, we are seeing much healthier pets walk into our surgery (and less often!!!).'

Birgit Ahlemeyer

• 'I qualified as a vet in 1973 and in all that time I have never come across such a useful, practical, sensible, clearly written book on how to feed your dog to achieve or maintain a perfect weight and perfect health.'

Richard Allport

- 'My 44 years in practice have convinced me that a good diet is critical to canine health. This excellent book shows how a natural diet can deal with obesity and maintain long-term health.'

Chris Almond

- 'Vicky's book is a great tool to help responsible pet owners improve their four-legged friend's health and fitness in a fun, natural and easy way that dogs will love. They cannot make their own choices, we do it for them, we are responsible for their welfare.'

Mar Alonso

- 'A very useful little book. If you have been struggling with getting your dog to lose weight this book will help you see a different path. A path that consistently creates happier, healthy dogs.'

Chris Aukland

- 'This book is a must for anyone struggling with an overweight dog. Vicky walks us through a practical, easy and healthy approach to weight loss. If you haven't already transitioned to a species-appropriate, raw-food diet, what are you waiting for?'

Reagan Carnwath

- 'Obesity is the number-one health issue affecting dogs in the UK. This superb little book is packed with simple, practical and effective advice to help you get the pounds off your pooches, and ensure they stay off.'

Neil Coode

• 'Precise and concise, naturally it's all you need to help your dog lose weight.'

Tim Couzens

• 'Obesity is one of the biggest health concerns in pets these days. The knock-on effects and secondary health concerns associated with obesity are staggering. This simple and well-written book gives such good, practical and healthy advice for owners and veterinary professionals alike. A must-read for anyone interested in helping their pet shed excess weight as well as to provide them with a much better quality of life and outlook for their future!'

Chelsea Dawson

• 'This book provides straightforward, easy to understand information on this important topic. A strongly recommended resource.'

Shelley Doxey

• 'It doesn't take long to realise that the reason feeding as nature intended works, is that it's what nature intended in the first place! Vicky's book is a great introduction for the beginner and will help you get started on a path you and your dog will never regret.'

Mark Elliott

- 'The Lucky Dog Weight Loss Plan is thoroughly researched and easy to follow. I am committed to raw feeding and find an increasing number of my clients are relieved when they discover I support this diet. I wish the book the success that it is due, with the aim to maintain optimum weights for pets of all ages and physical or medical conditions.'

  Robert Elliott

- 'What I love about this book is that it tells it as it is. You find out when, if and how to diet your dog in a natural way. I have dieted many dogs using this method, and they truly do lose weight in a healthy way – but there is also so much more information within this book about how to keep your dog happy and healthy, not just slim and trim. My most impressive case following this diet was a Labrador that went from 50kg to 32kg in a comfortable six months, having had limited success on commercial food (including commercial diet food). Well done Vicky for getting this out there to the public.'

  Tom Farrington

- 'I know dogs who have been on expensive dry diet food for years, been fed a fraction of the recommended amount, clearly felt they were being starved (and were), and never lost an ounce. After a change to raw food, they were clearly happy and satisfied – and the extra weight came off easily. Most people I know happily feed themselves and their kids, but get very worried about feeding their dog anything other than dog food in case they don't get the balance right. We don't get that alienated from common sense without some serious brainwashing from an industry with a product to sell. This book takes the reader by the hand and removes any worry.'

Lise Hansen

- 'I have been a vet for 27 years and this is one of the most important books about canine health I have ever read. It isn't just about how to get your dog to lose weight, it's about how to make your dog as well as it can be.'

Geoff Johnson

- 'At last, a common-sense, logical look at the increasing problem of obesity in our dogs. Vicky has written a great guide to natural feeding and weight loss in dogs that is easy to understand and to follow. Drawing on her enormous experience in this field she explains this approach to diet with humour but also with hard fact. I have encouraged hundreds of dog owners to change their dog's diet to a more natural one, and watched the astounding results of doing so. Not just weight loss, but also a huge return to health on every level. I shall be encouraging all my clients to read this book.'

Jane Keogh

• 'It never ceases to amaze me in general practice to what extent dog owners have lost complete touch with what their dogs can and should naturally eat. However, I find more and more of my clients querying the current general veterinary feeding advice. They wonder if it's really right to feed processed and dried kibble, sitting for weeks or even months in one's pantry, laced with taste improvers and other products even a dog would walk away from if offered a natural choice. After all, we all know what to feed ourselves and our children, the fresher and the more natural, the better! Vicky's book touches very well on the idea of 'natural nutrition' and the hows and whys. It rekindles the basic notion of what a dog actually should eat naturally. The book awakens thought processes needed to get back to knowing and understanding how nutrition is the basis for a healthy body. This book will help anyone on their way to providing the best nutrition for their dog! Let's hope more owners would grasp the need for common-sense dog feeding!'

Dorien F. Nel

• 'At last, a well-written book which addresses the growing problem of obesity in dogs. Clearly explaining the underlying causes of canine obesity and offering a simple and practical solution, every owner will gain new insights into the impact of diet on every aspect of their dog's life.'

Janet Nuttall

- 'As a vet, I am constantly encountering pets which are being suffocated with love, in the form of food! So it's fantastic to have a book which addresses the issues of canine obesity and health, and offers sensible advice and information regarding dieting and the general wellbeing of our much loved canine friends. A very worthwhile read even if your pet is not a little rounder than it should be!!'

Deeks Povah

- 'Feeding your dog a high-quality and well-balanced raw food diet could improve its wellbeing and ultimately lead to a happier, healthier pet. The Lucky Dog Weight Loss Plan provides practical advice to help you to achieve this.'

Nick Weston

Contact Information

Dr Birgit Ahlemeyer MRCVS
21 Post Horn Close, Forest Row, RH18 5DE
T: 01342 826104
E: birgitholisticvet@hotmail.co.uk

Dr Richard Allport BVetMed VetMFHom MRCVS
Natural Medicine Centre, 11 Southgate Road, Potters Bar,
Herts, EN6 5DR
T: 01707 662058
E: info@naturalmedicinecentre.net
W: www.naturalmedicinecentre.co.uk

Chris Almond BVSc. VetMFHom MRCVS
Forrest House Veterinary Group, 5 Little Market Place,
Masham, Ripon, North Yorkshire, HG4 4DY
T: 01765 689219

Dr Mar Alonso BVMS MRCVS VetLFHom Cert Vet Acu (IVAS)
Petersfield Centre for Integrated Veterinary Medicine,
22B High Street, Petersfield, Hampshire, GU32 3J
T: 01730 858160
E: petersfieldholisticvet@gmail.com
W: www.integratedveterinarymedicine.co.uk

Chris Aukland BVSc VetMFHom MRCVS
Forest Lodge Veterinary Centre, Station Road, Forest Row,
East Sussex, RH18 5DW
T: 01342 824452
E: chris.aukland@medivet.co.uk
W: www.medivet.co.uk/forestrow

Dr Reagan Carnwath BVMS MRCVS   Cert. IVAS Acupuncture
Herbal Vet Scotland, Unit 3, 5 Thornliebank Industrial Estate,
Glasgow, G46 8JH
T: 07786 381674
E: herbalvetscotland@gmail.com
W: www.herbalvetscotland.co.uk

Neil Coode BVSc MRCVS VetMFHom
Brookmead Vet Surgery, Horsham Road, Cranleigh,
Surrey, GU6 8DL
T: 01483 274242
E: info@brookmead-vets.co.uk
W: www.brookmead-vets.co.uk

Tim Couzens, BVetMed, MRCVS, VetMFHom, CertVetAc
The Holistic Veterinary Medicine Centre, The Village Works,
London Road, East Hoathly, Sussex BN8 6QA
T: 01825 840966
E: admin@hvmc.info
W: www.hvmc.info

Chelsea Dawson BVMS MRCVS GPCert WVA & CPM
Oakmount Veterinary Centre, Trafalgar St, Burnley, BB11 1TP
T: 01282 423 640
E: chelsea@oakmountvets.co.uk

Shelley Doxey BVetMed (Hons), MSc, BSc, MRCVS
Holistic Veterinary Care, Nr. Andover, Hants.
E: enquiries@shelleydoxey.co.uk
W: www.shelleydoxey.co.uk

Mark Elliott BVSc VetMFHom MRCVS MLIHM PCH DSH
RSHom
Mark Elliott and Associates, Madam Green Business Centre,
High Street, Oving, Chichester, West Sussex, PO20 2DD
T: 01243 779111
E: ovingvets@gmail.com
W: www.markelliott.co.uk

Robert Elliott B Vet Med, MRCVS
Robert Elliott Veterinary Surgery, 21–23 High Street, Stan-
ford-in-the-Vale, Oxfordshire SN7 8LH
T: 01367 710595

Tom Farrington MVB MRCVS VetMFHom
'Allswell', Barley Hill East, Rosscarbery, Co. Cork, Ireland
T: +353 (0)23 884 8811
E: farrington.vet@gmail.com

Lise Hansen DVM MRCVS CertIAVH PCH
& Andrew Prentis BVSc MRCVS
Hyde Park Veterinary Centre, 61 Connaught Street,
London W2 2AE
T: 020 7723 0453
W: www.hydeparkvet.co.uk

Geoff Johnson VetMB MA MRCVS VetMFHom RSHom PCH
Wiveliscombe Homeopathic And Homeopathic Vet Surgery,
12 North Street, Wiveliscombe, Somerset, TA4 2JY
T: 01984 624999
E: somersetvet@yahoo.com
W: www.vethomeopath.co.uk

Jane Keogh BVSc VetMFHom MRCVS
Southfield Veterinary Centre, 1 South Walks,
Dorchester, Dorset, DT1 1DU
T: 01305 262913
E: info@southfieldvet.co.uk & j.keogh5@btinternet.com

Dr Dorien F. Nel, DVM MRCVS
ODS Veterinary Services, 25 Avebury Road,
Chippenham, Wiltshire SN14 0NX
E: dorien_nel@hotmail.com

Janet Nuttall BVetMed MRCVS VetMFHom
Heathfield Vets, Chimneys, Hailsham Road,
Heathfield, East Sussex, TN21 8AD
T: 01435 864422
E: janet.nuttall@heathfieldvets.co.uk
W: www.heathfieldvets.co.uk

Deeks Povah BSc BVSc MRCVS
Vale Veterinary Centre,
Tiverton, Devon, EX16 4 LF
T: 01884 253355
E: valereception@btinternet.com

Nick Weston BVSc GPcert SAS EM&S MRCVS
Belmont Veterinary Clinic, Salisbury Road,
Pewsey, Wilts SN9 5PZ
T: 01672 563413
E: nick.weston@hungerfordvets.co.uk

14

MORE HELP IF YOU NEED IT

14

MORE HELP IF YOU NEED IT

This book is based on my own experience of feeding several thousand dogs a month using either the Lucky Dog Weight Loss Plan or a variation of it. When I first discovered all about the benefits of natural feeding (and the appalling damage being done by modern, processed food), I was so keen to spread the word that I couldn't decide whether to start a company or a cult. In the end I opted for a company – Honey's Real Dog Food – but I want to stress that the most important thing to me, and my colleagues, is canine health.

For this reason, we are happy to provide free unlimited advice and support to anyone who is interested in making the switch to a natural diet, even if they never plan to become a customer. We're especially pleased to help those caring for dogs with health issues or who are overweight.

Anyway, if you have any questions not answered in these pages please contact us (see below for contact information).

Meanwhile, this final chapter explains what we do at Honey's.

We Make Feeding A Natural Diet Incredibly Easy

At Honey's we make it incredibly easy to feed your dog

a natural diet. Our raw, fresh dog food is produced using lean, minced meat, which is certified organic, wild or free range. We offer a variety of seasonal recipes including chicken, pork, beef, turkey and lamb as well as wild rabbit and other game. You can opt for low fat as well as with and without vegetables. What about the all-important bone element – so crucial to your dog's health? We grind the bone (so that it can barely be seen) and mix it in. We also supply individual bones in convenient sizes as well as chicken wings, handmade biscuits and treats. I will come back to the subject in a moment, but I want to stress that we are deeply concerned about animal welfare and the environment. To the best of my knowledge, for instance, we are the only dog food producer in the UK that doesn't use any intensively reared meat. Incidentally, if you want to go the DIY route we can also help (see below).

A Very Personal Approach

One of the first things you'll notice if you decide to feed your dog Honey's is that we take a very personal approach. It isn't just that we want to know your dog's name; we also want to know his or her vital statistics, medical history, lifestyle, preferences and personality. We like a photograph, too, so that we can see what he or she looks like. Armed with the information you provide (together with your feedback), we can adjust the ingredients and quantities on an on-going basis so as to best meet your dog's needs.

The Ordering Process

We send our food, frozen, together with feeding notes, in recyclable boxes using an overnight delivery service. Our packaging keeps food cool for up to 48 hours. When your order arrives, we ask you to take it out of the box and put it into your freezer. We suggest that before going to bed every night you simply remove the following day's food from the freezer so that it has a chance to defrost. We ask you to keep us up to date with any changes in your dog's health or lifestyle so that we can adjust his or her diet if necessary. A week before we are due to make up the next month's supply we contact you to check everything we plan meets with your agreement, and then we repeat the whole process.

The first week of the Lucky Dog
Weight Loss Plan is free

Before I say another word, I just want to mention our
new customer offer. If you are based in the UK and
interested in trying our food out for a month we will
give you the first week free of charge. Alternatively,
new customers can try a smaller quantity of our food
with a half-price hamper.

Excellent Value For Money

It costs much less than you might expect to feed your dog with Honey's. We keep the cost down by dealing direct with our customers (so no profit to retailers or wholesalers). The price is linked to the exact weight of your dog and will be calculated for you as part of the order process. Our policy is to charge less than you would pay for the identical ingredients if you purchased them from an ethical supplier, such as Waitrose, Riverford or Able & Cole.

Our 100% Money-Back Guarantee

We are proud to say that almost all our customers come to us by word of mouth. In order to ensure that we maintain our reputation for quality, service and integrity we guarantee that your food will arrive in first-class condition on the promised date. If you are dissatisfied with the quality of our food, simply follow the instructions in the delivery box and we will refund the cost in full and without argument.

Never Worry About Running Out

Assuming you and your dog are happy with Honey's, we can set up a regular order for you so that you never have to worry about running out.

Our Chief Veterinary Surgeon Designs And Approves All Our Food

When you feed your dog Honey's you can rest assured that his or her diet has been designed and approved by our own Chief Veterinary Surgeon, Tom Farrington MVB MRCVS VetMFHom.

Tom is an honours veterinarian, holds an advanced degree in Veterinary Homeopathy, has over 30 years of experience in practice, lectures regularly and is responsible for creating an innovative range of homeopathic remedies called Homeopet (www.homeopet.com).

Tom has been encouraging owners to switch their dogs (and cats) to a raw food diet for over two decades. And in that time he has seen the practical benefits in thousands of cases.

Tom is responsible for devising all our formulas. He stipulates which ingredients should be used and in what proportions as well as providing guidance as to what volume of food should be fed each day. Thanks to him, you can be confident that Honey's Real Dog Food provides the right nutritional balance for your dog.

Free Veterinary Consultation, Without Obligation

If you are worried about your dog's health, a change of diet could really make a huge difference. A member of our Health Team (we employ our own vets, veterinary nurses and nutritionists) will be delighted to review your dog's health issues and make dietary recommendations. You will be under no obligation to accept their suggestions and no charge will be made. Where our consultant recommends a raw diet (and this isn't automatic, as they are all completely independent), we will happily quote for preparing it for you.

We Are Deeply Concerned About Animal Welfare

All the meat we use is free-range and/or certified organic or (in the case of the game) wild. We are concerned about the welfare of the animals we use to make our food. We know and trust all the farmers we buy from. Our objective is to keep 'dog food miles' to a minimum. We try to source everything from local, ethical farmers. By 'local', we mean as close to our kitchens in Pewsey as possible. When ingredients are hard to source locally we may have to go further afield (up to Wales or Scotland, for instance). We never source ingredients that are not from mainland Britain. We won't touch factory-farmed animals.

All Our Dog Food Is Suitable For Human Consumption

It isn't just that our ingredients must pass the 'suitable for human consumption' test: they must be of the highest quality we can find. We don't buy any ingredients that we wouldn't be happy to cook for our own families.

About The Business

Our kitchens are based in the depths of rural Wiltshire and we source our ingredients from small, local suppliers.

Our offices are just up the lane from my home and so you may sometimes hear dogs and children in the background when you call. We aren't a big venture and this allows us to offer a genuinely personal service. In fact, we must be the only dog food company in the world that knows just about every single one of its canine customers by name.

We Donate 1% Of Sales To Compassion In World Farming

We donate 1% of all our sales to Compassion in World Farming (CIWF). This is because we believe that the low standard of farm animal welfare both in the UK and elsewhere is one of the greatest scandals in modern human history. CIWF was founded in 1967 by a British farmer who became horrified by the development of modern, intensive factory farming. Today it strives peacefully to end all cruel factory farming practices. Its campaigning has resulted in the EU recognising animals as sentient beings, capable of feeling pain and suffering. It has also secured landmark agreements to outlaw the barren battery cage for egg-laying hens, narrow veal crates and sow stalls across Europe. We like the fact that CIWF generally works with business, not against it.

Just Looking For Ethically Sourced Ingredients?

If you want to prepare your own raw food then we can supply you with a range of ethically sourced raw ingredients along with full instructions.

The choice changes according to the season but generally includes carcasses (chicken, turkey, duck etc.), raw meaty bones, heart (ox, lamb, beef etc.), liver, tripe (washed in water), chicken wings, necks (chicken, turkey etc.) and even sheep heads.

If you are new to raw feeding, we usually recommend that you begin with our complete food and then, once you have got the hang of it, start to make the switch. All our raw ingredients are suitable for human consumption.

Please, Please Remember We Are Happy To Offer Free Advice

Our main objective at Honey's is to encourage people to switch their dogs to a natural diet. We will happily help you with free advice, tips and recipes even if there is never, ever any chance that you will become a customer. Please don't hesitate to contact us if you feel we can help you.

THE LUCKY DOG WEIGHT LOSS PLAN

How To Get In Touch With Honey's

By telephone
+ 44 (0)1672 620 260

By email
info@honeysrealdogfood.com

By post
Honey's Real Dog Food
Darling's House
1–3 Salisbury Road
Pewsey
Wiltshire SN9 5PZ
England

Or visit our website
www.honeysrealdogfood.com

FURTHER READING

FURTHER READING

'Outside of a dog,' advised Groucho Marx, 'a book is man's best friend. Inside of a dog it's too dark to read.' Quite where that leaves books about dogs' insides I am not entirely sure, but here are details of my favourites (in no particular order).

Dr. Becker's Real Food for Healthy Dogs & Cats
Beth Taylor and Karen Shaw Becker
- A brilliant explanation as to why dogs should be eating a natural diet, with lots of recipes

Dogs, Diet and Disease
Caroline Levin
- This book explains how canine metabolism and endocrine functions work in a normal dog. A relatively plain-English guide to your dog's innards

Foods Pets Die For: Shocking Facts About Pet Foods
Ann N. Martin
- The title says it all. Martin exposes the dog food industry for what it is

Give Your Dog a Bone
Dr Ian Billinghurst
- The first popular book to promote the idea of feeding dogs raw food and meaty bones. Its author is considered one of the world's leading experts on the subject

Grow Your Pups with Bones
Dr Ian Billinghurst
- Aimed at breeders, this book contains lots of useful information on feeding pregnant mums, new mums and puppies

Honey's Natural Feeding Handbook for Dogs
Jonathan Self
- Written by my co-founder at Honey's. I cover much of the same ground in this book but if you want a plain-English guide to the subject there isn't a better one

Natural Nutrition for Dogs and Cats
Kathy Schultze
- A comprehensive raw feeding guide. Schultze takes a strong line on certain ingredients (such as dairy and honey) which I am more relaxed about

Pottenger's Cats: A Study in Nutrition
Frances Pottenger
- Dr Pottenger discovered, quite by accident, that cats' health degenerated unless they were fed raw food. In his 10-year study of 900 cats, he found the optimal diet for his cats was two-thirds raw meat and one-third raw milk, plus a little cod liver oil

Raw Food for Dogs: The Ultimate Reference for Dog Owners!
Mogens Eliasen
 • Available online. An easy read and packed with useful information and research

Raw Meaty Bones: Promote Health
Tom Lonsdale
 • Lonsdale has fought a long and bloody battle with the various veterinary professional bodies over canine and feline diet. This book describes his campaign and offers practical advice

Raw & Natural Nutrition for Dogs
Lew Olson
 • A plain-English approach to quite complicated subjects (well, complicated if one only just scraped through biology at school)

Real Food for Dogs and Cats
Dr Clare Middle
 • This book is short and well written and provides a comprehensive and easy-to-understand guide to raw feeding. Contains details of relevant raw feeding research

Ruined by Excess: Perfected by Lack: The Paradox of Pet Nutrition
Richard Patton

- An expert in canine nutrition, Patton provides plenty of scientific evidence to back up his claims that canine health is being ruined by modern dog food

Unlocking the Canine Ancestral Diet
Steve Brown

- This book contains fascinating original research into what dogs would eat in the wild and how best to replicate it using 'domestic' ingredients

Good Money: Become an Ethical Entrepreneur. Change the World. Feel Better
Jonathan Self

- This book is all about how to start an ethical business (and why you might want to do it) using Honey's Real Dog Food as the main example. If you are interested in our business model, which puts principles before profits, then I can really recommend this business

THE LUCKY DOG FOOD DIARY

Use the following pages to
record what your Lucky Dog
is consuming...

Week 1

Commencing Monday _____ of _____
Weekly weigh-in details:
Dog's weight _____ kg _____ g

Food Record

	Daily food Record	Accidental food intake	Exercise
MON			
TUE			
WED			
THU			
FRI			
SAT			
SUN			

Week 2

Commencing Monday _____ of _____
Weekly weigh-in details:
Dog's weight _____ kg _____ g

Food Record

	Daily food Record	Accidental food intake	Exercise
MON			
TUE			
WED			
THU			
FRI			
SAT			
SUN			

Week 3

Commencing Monday _____ of _____
Weekly weigh-in details:
Dog's weight _____ kg _____g

Food Record

	Daily food Record	Accidental food intake	Exercise
MON			
TUE			
WED			
THU			
FRI			
SAT			
SUN			

Week 4

Commencing Monday _____ of _____
Weekly weigh-in details:
Dog's weight _____ kg _____g

Food Record

	Daily food Record	Accidental food intake	Exercise
MON			
TUE			
WED			
THU			
FRI			
SAT			
SUN			

Week 5

Commencing Monday ____ of _____
Weekly weigh-in details:
Dog's weight _____ kg _____g

Food Record

	Daily food Record	Accidental food intake	Exercise
MON			
TUE			
WED			
THU			
FRI			
SAT			
SUN			

Week 6

Commencing Monday ____ of _____
Weekly weigh-in details:
Dog's weight _____ kg _____ g

Food Record

	Daily food Record	Accidental food intake	Exercise
MON			
TUE			
WED			
THU			
FRI			
SAT			
SUN			